fabulous desserts to make you famous

by YVONNE YOUNG TARR

CITADEL PRESS   SECAUCUS, N.J.

Also by Yvonne Young Tarr

The Ten-Minute Gourmet Cookbook
The Ten-Minute Diet Cookbook
Love Portions
The New York Times Bread and Soup Cookbook
The Complete Outdoor Cookbook
The New York Times Farmhouse Cookbook
The Super-Easy Step-by-Step Wine Making Book
The Super-Easy Step-by-Step Sausage Making Book
The Super-Easy Step-by-Step Cheese Making Book
The Super-Easy Step-by-Step Book of Special Breads
The Up With Wholesome, Down With Store-Bought Book of
    Formulas and Recipes
The Tomato Book
The New Ten-Minute Gourmet Cookbook

---

introduction

This book has one objective . . . to make you famous for your desserts.

The recipes that follow have all been chosen for their star quality. They are meant to be—and are—spectacular desserts for special occasions . . . beautiful and dramatic conversation pieces! Flaming crêpes, creamy soufflés, frozen mousses, tortes, steamed puddings, cheesecakes, out-of-this-world pies, éclairs, cream puffs, rum cakes, icebox cakes, trifles, ladyfinger cakes—each delicately flavored and creatively decorated—will grace your table and leave your guests smiling with satisfaction and admiration.

The following recipes have another important asset. Each is completely reliable. I have personally tested and retested every one in my own kitchen on cooking equipment similar to yours.

Any recipe that proved tricky or temperamental (such as meringues that go all horrible on extra-damp days) has been unceremoniously shown the kitchen door. If you are a normally good cook, there is not one recipe in this book that you cannot prepare to perfection time after time.

Many of these desserts are time consuming, some are expensive to prepare, but this is the price for fame. Few, if any, accomplishments are achieved without payment of some kind on our part. The reward for the investment of time and care is, in this case, heady indeed. You will henceforth and forever be known as . . . "The one who makes those fantastic desserts!"

Oven temperatures:

300° F. to 350° F.—Low
350° F. to 400° F.—Medium
400° F. to 450° F.—High

I dedicate this book to
two remarkable women . . . my mother, Margaret Young,
and my mother-in-law, Hannah Tarr.

(With special thanks to Toni, Patty, and Jonathan)

contents

desserts to serve eight persons

Eight seems to be the magic number when dinner parties are being planned. Consequently nearly half of the recipes in this book are devoted to the care and feeding of precisely that number of guests.

Some of the recipes in this section are generous enough to serve nine or even ten persons, and these are so indicated. However, for guests with extra-large appetites, I would suggest a dessert from that portion of this book devoted to "Desserts to Serve Ten to Twelve Persons."

skillet
strawberry
shortcake

(Serves 8)

The basis for this attractive dessert is a perfect, slightly sweetened, skillet-baked shortcake. Just split the cake, fill with strawberries and whipped cream, top with the same, and "Voila!" you're famous for your strawberry shortcake.

Ingredients

2 Cups all-purpose flour
¼ Cup plus 1 tablespoon granulated sugar
1 Tablespoon plus 1 teaspoon baking powder
½ Teaspoon salt
6 Tablespoons butter
2 Eggs
¼ Cup milk
3 Tablespoons butter
2 Quarts strawberries
¾ Cup granulated sugar
1 Teaspoon lemon juice
1 Cup heavy cream
2 Tablespoons granulated sugar
1 Teaspoon vanilla

Directions

Place a mixing bowl in the refrigerator to chill for use later on. Sift together the first four ingredients. With a pastry cutter or two knives, cut in 6 tablespoons of butter to produce a mealy mixture. Beat the eggs and the milk together and stir in the sifted dry ingredients. Mix thoroughly to make a soft dough. (If the dough is too sticky, add 1 tablespoon of flour and mix again.) Turn the dough onto a floured surface and pat into a thick circle about 9 inches in diameter. Grease a heavy 9-inch skillet and press the dough to fit. Bake at 375 degrees F. for 28 minutes or until golden brown. Remove the shortcake from the pan and place it on a wire rack to cool slightly. Split the shortcake into two layers and spread the inside surfaces with butter. Wash, stem, and slice one quart of the strawberries. Add ¾ cup granulated sugar and the lemon juice. Crush slightly and chill. Wash, stem, and cut into halves the remaining one quart of berries. Chill. Remove the bowl and the heavy cream from the refrigerator. Whip the cream with the sugar and vanilla. Place the whipped cream in the refrigerator.

TO SERVE

Place the bottom layer of the shortcake on a serving plate and cover with crushed berries and half the whipped cream. Top this with the other half of the shortcake, slather this with the remaining whipped cream, and decorate with the remaining strawberries. Serve immediately.

apple shortcake with lemon sauce

(Serves 8)

Plain and fancy meet in this rich, crumbly shortcake that is covered with spicy, cooked apple slices, and topped with tart lemon sauce. A slightly different dessert to serve with any meal that is as American as apple pie.

APPLE FILLING
Ingredients

2¼ Cups water	¼ Teaspoon nutmeg
1¼ Cups granulated sugar	7 Medium-sized McIntosh apples

Directions

Bring the water, the sugar, and the nutmeg to a boil in a medium-sized saucepan. Boil, stirring, for 5 minutes. Peel, core, and quarter the apples. Add them to the syrup and poach gently until they are tender, but not mushy. Using a slotted spoon, scoop the fruit from the syrup, place in an ovenproof bowl, and cool to room temperature. Boil the syrup remaining in the pan until it is reduced to ¾ cup. Cool.

SHORTCAKE
Ingredients

2 Cups all-purpose flour
¼ Cup plus 1 tablespoon granulated sugar
1 Tablespoon plus 1 teaspoon baking powder
½ Teaspoon salt

6 Tablespoons butter
2 Eggs
¼ Cup milk

Directions

Sift together the first four ingredients. With a pastry blender or two knives, cut in the butter to produce a mealy mixture. Beat the eggs and the milk together, and stir in the sifted dry ingredients. Mix thoroughly to make a soft dough. (If the dough is too sticky to handle, add 1 tablespoon of flour and mix again.) Turn the dough onto a floured surface and pat into a thick circle about 9 inches in diameter. Grease a heavy 9-inch skillet and press the dough to fit. Bake at 375 degrees F. for 28 minutes or until golden brown. Remove the shortcake from the pan and place it on a wire rack to cool slightly. Split the cake into two layers and spread the inside surfaces with butter.

LEMON SAUCE
Ingredients

2 Lemons
4 Tablespoons butter

1 Cup granulated sugar
2 Eggs

Directions

Use a fine grater to grate the *yellow* rind from the lemons. (Do not include any of the white inner rind or the sauce will be bitter.) Squeeze the juice from the lemons. Place the grated rind, lemon juice, butter and sugar in the top of a double boiler and stir over boiling water, until the sugar is completely dissolved. Turn the flame to low. Beat the eggs and stir them into the lemon mixture. Continue to cook, stirring constantly, until the mixture thickens slightly. *Do not allow to boil,* or the sauce will curdle. Cool slightly.

TO ASSEMBLE

Spread the cooled apples on the bottom half of the cake. Spoon the cooled apple syrup over the apples. Turn the top half of the shortcake onto this and serve at once, topped with warm Lemon Sauce.

13

pêches flambées

In this exciting dessert, fresh, ripe peach halves are poached in syrup, set like golden crowns on mounds of macaroon crumbs, and flamed with Cointreau.

Ingredients

8 Fully ripe peaches
1½ Cups water
1½ Cups granulated sugar
2 Teaspoons lemon juice
32 Tablespoons macaroon crumbs (approximately 2¼ cups)
½ Cup Cointreau

Directions

Place peaches in a Pyrex bowl. Cover with boiling water. Lift out one peach, cut it in half, and carefully remove the pit. Gently pull off the skin with a paring knife. Repeat the process with the remaining peaches. Place 1½ cups of boiling water and 1½ cups of sugar in a saucepan. Boil over a high flame. Add peach halves and lemon juice, and boil for 4 minutes. Meanwhile, make 2 mounds of macaroon crumbs on eight small serving plates. Each mound should consist of two tablespoons of macaroon crumbs. Place the peaches and syrup in a blazer pan of a chafing dish. Arrange serving plates with macaroon crumbs on a tray. When ready to serve, carry chafing dish and the serving plates to the table. Heat peaches and syrup over medium flame. Heat the Cointreau slightly and set it aflame. Spoon the flaming Cointreau over the peaches in the syrup. Place a peach half on each mound of macaroon crumbs. Spoon several tablespoonfuls of Cointreau syrup mixture over each peach half. Serve warm.

cherries jubilee

A flaming dessert seems to make a meal especially exciting. It is desirable, however, for the flavor of the flaming aftermath to be equal to its pyrotechnic beauty. Such is most definitely the case in this classic dessert.

Ingredients

2 Pounds fresh Bing cherries
2 Cups water
¾ Cup granulated sugar
¼ Cup Cherry Marnier or Cherry Heering
1 Teaspoon cornstarch
1 Tablespoon water
2 Quarts vanilla ice cream
16 Drops red food coloring
1 Cup whipped cream
¼ Cup kirsch or Cherry Marnier or Cherry Heering

Directions

Wash the cherries, pit them, and remove any stems. In a saucepan, place half the pitted cherries, the water, the sugar and ¼ cup Cherry Marnier. Simmer gently for 5 minutes, stirring occasionally. Mix the cornstarch with 1 tablespoon of water, stir in a little of the cherry juice, and stir the mixture into the cooked cherries. Add the remaining cherries and bring the mixture to a boil, stirring constantly. When the sauce has thickened slightly, reduce the heat and simmer for 2 minutes. Remove from the heat and reserve for later use.

Soften the ice cream slightly, and stir the food coloring into it. Place the ice cream in a decorative mold and refreeze. One hour prior to serving, unmold the ice cream onto a plate and decorate it with whipped cream piped through a pastry tube. Freeze until time to serve. At that time, heat the cherries and place them in the top of a chafing dish. Carry the hot cherries and the molded ice cream to the table. Pour over the cherries the kirsch or Cherry Marnier or Cherry Heering. Heat slightly and blaze. Cut the ice cream and cover with the hot cherries. Serve immediately.

cherry pudding

Have you ever tasted a pudding so rich and crumbly that it is very nearly a cake? If not, you really should try this one.

Ingredients

2 Cups all-purpose flour
4 Tablespoons granulated sugar
2 Teaspoons baking powder
1 Teaspoon salt
3 Tablespoons butter
⅔ Cup milk

1 Egg
1 ⅔ Cups pitted,
   tart canned cherries, drained
1 Cup granulated sugar
¼ Cup Cherry Marnier

Directions

Sift the flour, the 4 tablespoons sugar, the baking powder, and the salt into a bowl. Using two knives or a pastry blender, cut the butter into the flour until the mixture is mealy. Beat the milk and egg together. Stir into the flour mixture. Spread this thick batter on a buttered 9-inch cake pan. Boil the drained cherries, 1 cup sugar, and Cherry Marnier until the mixture is syrupy and rather thick. Spread this cherry mixture on the batter in the pan. Bake for 30 minutes in an oven preheated to 375 degrees F. Serve warm with hot sauce.

HOT BRANDY SAUCE
Ingredients

¼ Cup granulated sugar
2 Tablespoons all-purpose flour
1½ Cups boiling water
3 Tablespoons butter

½ Teaspoon salt
2 Tablespoons brandy
¼ Cup heavy cream
1 Teaspoon vanilla

Directions

Mix the sugar and flour in a saucepan. Stir in the boiling water. Cook until this mixture is smooth and begins to bubble. Stir in the butter, the salt, and the brandy. Boil gently for three minutes more. Stir in the cream and the vanilla. Serve hot.

carrot cake

(Serves 8)

Who would ever expect the lowly carrot to come to the dinner table dressed as a dessert? Well, here it does just that, and does so deliciously.

CAKE

Ingredients

⅔ Cup finely grated raw carrot
⅔ Cup finely grated
   blanched almonds

1¼ Cups granulated sugar
8 Eggs
⅛ Teaspoon cinnamon

Directions

Measure the grated carrots and the grated almonds. Separate the egg yolks from the whites. Beat the sugar and the egg yolks in a bowl until the mixture is thick and creamy. Add the grated carrots, the grated almonds, and the cinnamon. Beat the egg whites until they stand in stiff peaks, and fold them carefully into the carrot-nut mixture. Butter two shallow 9-inch square cake pans. Turn ½ the batter into each pan. Smooth the top lightly. Bake for 1 hour in an oven preheated to 275 degrees F. Cool the layers and turn one onto a glass cake plate. Spread this with orange marmalade, and top with the second layer. Serve with Rum Custard.

RUM CUSTARD

Ingredients

4 Eggs
½ Cup granulated sugar
1 Cup milk

½ Cup heavy cream
1 Tablespoon rum

Directions

Beat the eggs in the top of a double boiler. Add the sugar and continue beating until thoroughly mixed. Scald the milk and heavy cream, and pour this mixture gradually into the eggs, stirring constantly. Place the mixture over simmering water and stir until it thickens slightly. Do not overcook or the custard will curdle. Place the pan in cold water for a few seconds, and then stir in the rum. Chill the custard, stirring occasionally.

fruit compote[*]

(Serves 8)

A fruit compote is the perfect aftermath to an especially rich meal.

1 Cup Cointreau
½ Cup water
* 1 Cup dried apricots
½ Cup golden raisins
1 Vanilla bean
4 Ripe pineapples
2 Cups peeled peach slices
¾ Cup honey
¼ Cup fresh lime juice
1 Cup Bing cherries halved and pitted

Directions

Mix the Cointreau and the water in a large bowl. Wash the apricots and place them in the Cointreau mixture. Refrigerate for two days. On the morning of the second day, stir the raisins and the seeds from the vanilla bean into the apricots. Refrigerate until serving time. Cut the pineapples with their leaves in half lengthwise. Cut out the fruit and the cores, leaving eight ½-inch-thick shells. Place the shells in the refrigerator until serving time. Discard the core and cut the pineapple meat into bite-size pieces. Drain the liquid from the apricots and raisins and stir into them the pineapple pieces, the peeled peach slices, the honey, and the lime juice. Chill for at least one hour. At serving time toss the Bing cherry halves with the other fruit, pile the compote into the pineapple shells. Serve cold.

* Prepare the apricots 2 days in advance of serving.

toasted almond cream

(Serves 8)

Have you ever tasted "crunchy" cream? If not, here's your chance.

Ingredients

8 Egg yolks
1 Cup granulated sugar
2 Cups milk
1 Teaspoon vanilla extract
2 Tablespoons rum
3 Tablespoons unflavored gelatin
⅓ Cup water
2 Tablespoons butter
1 Cup almonds
3 Ounces chilled semi-sweet chocolate
2 Cups heavy cream

Directions

Place the egg yolks and the sugar in the top of a double boiler. Beat until light and creamy. Gradually stir in the milk and cook the mixture over boiling water until it begins to thicken. Remove from the heat and stir in the vanilla extract and the rum. Soften the gelatin in ⅓ cup of water and stir it into the hot custard until the gelatin is dissolved. Chill until the mixture begins to set. Melt the butter on a baking sheet, stir in the chopped nuts, and toast them under the broiler, stirring frequently. Use a sharp knife to shave bits of the chilled chocolate. Do not allow the chocolate bits to melt. Whip the cream until stiff and fold it with the nuts, and the chocolate bits, into the custard. Lightly oil a mold, pour in the almond cream, and chill it for 2 to 3 hours. Unmold the cream onto a cold silver platter. Pipe points of whipped cream around the bottom of the dessert, shave chocolate bits onto the top of it, and decorate with whole almonds, standing at attention around the outer edge. Serve very cold.

victorian cream with crème de menthe

(Serves 8 to 10)

An unexpected combination of flavors makes this a dessert your guests will not soon forget. Two rich and smooth-textured creams, one vanilla and one chocolate, are chilled, unmolded, and splashed with crème de menthe. "Cool on cool" it might be called.

VANILLA CREAM

Ingredients

1 Tablespoon unflavored gelatin
2½ Tablespoons cold water
1 Cup heavy cream
½ Cup plus 1 tablespoon granulated sugar
1 Cup sour cream
1 Teaspoon vanilla extract

Directions

Sprinkle the gelatin over the cold water to soften. Stir the heavy cream and the sugar over a low flame until the sugar is dissolved. Remove from the flame and add the softened gelatin. Stir until the gelatin is completely dissolved. Add the sour cream and the vanilla and mix thoroughly. Pour the cream into a six-cup mold. Chill for two hours.

CHOCOLATE CREAM

Ingredients

1 Tablespoon plus 1 teaspoon unflavored gelatin
3 Tablespoons cold water
4 Ounces semi-sweet chocolate
1 Cup milk
½ Cup granulated sugar
3 Egg yolks
1 Cup sour cream
1 Teaspoon vanilla extract

Directions

Sprinkle the gelatin over the cold water to soften. Melt the chocolate in one cup of milk, mixed with ½ cup of sugar. (Be sure that the chocolate is *completely* melted.) Dissolve the softened gelatin in the hot chocolate mixture. Beat the egg yolks lightly and pour them into the chocolate, in a thin stream, stirring constantly. Add the sour cream and the vanilla, and mix thoroughly. Cool to room temperature. When the vanilla cream has set, pour the chocolate cream onto it and chill for 2 hours more, or until the cream has completely set. Unmold onto a serving plate.

TO SERVE

Ingredients

½ Cup heavy cream
2 Tablespoons granulated sugar
¼ Cup crème de menthe

Directions

Whip the heavy cream with the sugar until it is quite stiff. Use a pastry tube to pipe the whipped cream in arabesques and rosettes around the base of the molded Victorian Cream. Dribble the crème de menthe over the sides of the mold.

gâteau
saint-honoré

A very special cake for very special occasions is Gâteau Saint-Honoré. A cream-puff ring is placed on a base of tart pastry. This ring is filled with a frothy Crème Saint-Honoré, and the same delicious cream is heaped high in the center of the cake. Tiny cream puffs and marrons glacé are arranged around the top, and whipped cream is piped around these for a final touch. The cake is time consuming, but not tricky, to make. Why not create it for your next dinner party?

TART PASTRY
Ingredients

1 Cup presifted all-purpose flour	½ Cup butter
¼ Teaspoon salt	3 or 4 Tablespoons ice water

Directions

Sift the flour and the salt into a mixing bowl. Cut in the butter with a pastry blender or two knives until the mixture has the consistency of corn meal. Add the remaining butter and blend until the particles are the size of small peas. Sprinkle in the ice water and stir with a fork until the pastry forms a ball. Refrigerate for 10 minutes. Roll out the pastry on a lightly floured surface to a circle 9 inches in diameter. Press this into the bottom of a 9-inch spring-form pan. Prepare Pâte à Choux.

PÂTE À CHOUX
Ingredients

1 Cup water	1¼ Cups all-purpose flour
½ Cup butter	5 Eggs

Directions

Boil the water and butter together in a saucepan. Add the flour, all at one time, and stir rapidly with a wooden spoon until the dough leaves the sides of the pan and forms a ball. Remove the pan from the heat and beat in the eggs, one at a time, beating after each addition. Continue beating until the mixture is smooth and has a sheen. Use a pastry tube without the nozzle to pipe one-half the Pâte à Choux, 2 inches high, around the inside edge of the pan. Bake the Pâte à Choux for 15 minutes at 425 degrees F.; then lower the heat to 375 degrees F. and bake until they are golden brown and the sides feel rigid (approximately 15 to 20 minutes). Remove from the oven and set aside to cool.

CRÈME SAINT-HONORÉ
Ingredients

7 Egg yolks	2 Tablespoons Cointreau
2½ Cups milk	1 Cup heavy cream
1¼ Cups granulated sugar	3 Tablespoons granulated sugar
½ Cup all-purpose flour	1 10-Ounce jar marrons glacés
2 Tablespoons unflavored gelatin	or 12 candied cherries
¼ Cup water	

Directions

Beat the egg yolks in the top of a large double boiler. Add the 1¼ cups of granulated sugar and beat the mixture until it is fluffy and light in color. Add the flour and mix well. Scald the milk and pour it over the egg mixture a little at a time, stirring constantly until it is well blended. Place over boiling water and cook, stirring continually until the mixture is smooth and thickened. Do not allow the cream to come to a boil. Remove from the heat. Soften the gelatin in the water and stir this into the hot custard. Cool the custard and stir in the Cointreau. Place the custard in the refrigerator until it begins to set. Meanwhile, whip the heavy cream until it thickens slightly. Sprinkle in the 3 table-spoons granulated sugar, beating constantly, until the cream is quite stiff. Remove the chilled custard from the refrigerator and fold in half of the whipped cream. Fill the cream puffs with this Crème Saint-Honoré and set them aside. Heap the remaining Crème Saint-Honoré into the center of the cooled, baked puff ring. Chill the cake and the puffs for 3 hours. To assemble the cake, arrange the cream puffs around the edge of the cake. Set the marrons glacés or candied cherries between them. Pipe a decorative edge of the remaining whipped cream around the puffs and on the top of the cake. Chill for several more hours, and serve cold.

orange cream torte

(Serves 8)

Here crunchy rolled-oat layers join forces with smooth orange cream to produce an unusual and delicate dessert.

ROLLED OAT LAYERS

Ingredients

7 Tablespoons butter
½ Teaspoon nutmeg
1¼ Cups old-fashioned rolled oats
1 Tablespoon all-purpose flour
1 Tablespoon grated orange zest (orange-colored outside layer of orange skin grated without including any of the bitter white inner skin)
1 Teaspoon baking powder
1 Egg
⅔ Cup granulated sugar

Directions

Melt the butter and place it in a large bowl with the nutmeg and the rolled oats. Stir. Sprinkle the flour, the orange zest, and the baking powder over this. Mix well. In a small bowl beat the egg and the sugar until they are fluffy and then beat these into the dry ingredients. Butter and flour the bottoms of three 9-inch spring-form pans (or the backs of three 9-inch cake pans). Spread the batter on them to within one inch of the edges of the pans. Bake for 15 minutes in an oven preheated to 350 degrees F. Turn off the oven flame, open the oven door, and remove one pan. Allow the other two layers to remain in the hot oven while you remove the first layer from the pan with a sharp knife. Remove the other layers, one at a time, and cool them on a flat surface.

ORANGE CREAM
Ingredients

¼ Cup granulated sugar
2½ Teaspoons potato starch
2 Egg yolks
¼ Cup apricot jam or preserves

1¼ Cups milk
1 Cup orange juice
⅓ Cup cold water
2 Envelopes unflavored gelatin

Directions

Mix the sugar, the potato starch, and the egg yolks in the saucepan. Stir in the apricot jam. Add the milk and the orange juice, a little at a time. Cook over low heat, stirring constantly, until the mixture thickens. Soften the gelatin in the cold water, add it to the hot orange mixture, and stir until the gelatin is dissolved. Chill but do not allow to set completely.

TO ASSEMBLE THE TORTE
Ingredients

2 Cups heavy cream
¼ Cup granulated sugar
1 Can mandarin orange sections

Directions

Whip one cup cream until it is stiff, and fold it into the chilled, unset orange cream. Chill once again until this orange cream filling is almost set, and spread it between the layers of the torte. Chill the torte until the cream is completely set. Whip the remaining cup of heavy cream with the sugar until it is stiff, and use this to "ice" the top of the torte. If any orange cream filling has fallen from between the layers use a spatula to smooth it in and around the torte. Use a pastry bag with a fancy tube to pipe rosettes around the top of the torte. Drain the mandarin sections well and arrange them decoratively around the whipped cream rosettes. Chill the torte for four hours before serving.

vanilla and chocolate soufflé

(Serves 4)

Filed under "luscious" in my files is this recipe for a creamy Vanilla and Chocolate Soufflé. (To serve 8, double the ingredients and bake in two soufflé dishes.)

VANILLA SOUFFLÉ
Ingredients

1½ Tablespoons butter	¼ Cup granulated sugar
1 Tablespoon all-purpose flour	2-Inch piece of vanilla bean
½ Cup milk	2 Egg yolks
⅛ Teaspoon salt	3 Egg whites

Directions

Melt the butter in a small skillet, add the flour, and blend until smooth. Add the milk, a little at a time, stirring constantly. Mix in the salt, the sugar, and the split vanilla bean. Cook until the sauce is thick and smooth. Cool to room temperature. Beat the egg yolks lightly and add them to the sauce. Beat well. Remove the vanilla bean. Beat the egg whites until they are stiff, and carefully fold them into the sauce.

CHOCOLATE SOUFFLÉ
Ingredients

1½ Tablespoons butter
1 Tablespoon all-purpose flour
½ Cup milk
1 Square semi-sweet chocolate
⅛ Teaspoon salt

¼ Cup granulated sugar
1-Inch piece of vanilla bean
2 Egg yolks
3 Egg whites

Directions

Melt the butter in a small skillet, add the flour, and blend until smooth. Add the milk, a little at a time, stirring constantly. Add the chocolate and stir until it has melted completely and the sauce is thoroughly blended. Mix in the salt, the sugar, and the split vanilla bean. Cook until the sauce is thick and smooth. Cool to room temperature. Beat the egg yolks lightly and add them to the sauce. Beat well. Remove the vanilla bean. Beat the egg whites until they are stiff and carefully fold them into the sauce.

Butter a soufflé dish and sprinkle it with sugar. Spoon in the two soufflé batters side by side. Place the soufflé dish in a pan of hot, not boiling, water. Bake for 15 minutes in an oven preheated to 400 degrees F. Reduce the heat to 375 degrees F. and cook for 20 minutes more. Serve immediately.

VARIATIONS

All-chocolate or all-vanilla soufflés may be prepared by doubling either recipe. Soufflés may be served with dessert sauces or with whipped cream. A really good soufflé, however, needs no embellishment.

cold
orange
blossom
soufflé

(Serves 8)

This cool, fluffy orange soufflé is an ideal dessert to grace any summer dinner party.

Ingredients

3 Tablespoons unflavored gelatin
1¾ Cups cold water
½ Cup granulated sugar
12 Ounces frozen orange juice concentrate
1 Eleven-ounce can mandarin orange segments in light syrup
⅓ Cup Cointreau
2 Cups heavy cream
4 Tablespoons granulated sugar

Directions

In a 3-quart saucepan soften the gelatin in the cold water and stir over low heat until the gelatin is completely dissolved. Remove from the heat, add the ½ cup of sugar, and stir until the sugar is dissolved. Add the unthawed orange juice concentrate and stir until it is melted. Stir in the Cointreau and the syrup drained from the mandarin oranges. Chill until the mixture consistency is slightly thicker than that of unbeaten egg white. Meanwhile, beat the heavy cream until it begins to thicken, sprinkle in the sugar, and continue to beat until the cream is stiff. Reserve ¼ cup of whipped cream and fold the rest into the slightly thickened gelatin-orange mixture. Tie a high collar of lightly oiled wax paper around the outside of a one-quart soufflé dish. Chill until firm. To serve remove the wax paper and garnish with the mandarin orange sections and small white whipped cream "blossoms."

chocolate fondue

(Serves 8)

For a luscious dessert that is easy to prepare and fun to eat, simply dip tasty tidbits into this creamy chocolate fondue.

Ingredients

18 Ounces Swiss milk chocolate (if Swiss chocolate is not available, substitute any fine quality milk chocolate)
1 Cup heavy cream
8 Tablespoons kirsch
1½ Cups small ripe strawberries
1½ Cups ripe pear slices
2 Cups 1-inch pieces angel food cake
¾ Cup golden raisins
¾ Cup candied cherries
Or bits of pineapple, maraschino cherries, tangerine sections, miniature cream puffs, nuts, etc. In fact, almost any tidbit that tastes good when it is chocolate covered may be served with chocolate fondue.

Directions

Break the chocolate into pieces and place these pieces, with the heavy cream, in a small chafing dish. Melt the chocolate over a low flame, stirring constantly. Stir in the kirsch and continue to cook for one minute. Serve the fondue in the chafing dish surrounded by small bowls of tidbits. To eat, spear bits of fruit, etc., with fondue forks and dip them into the melted chocolate. If chocolate cools, reheat.

chocolate-iced cheesecake

(Serves 8 to 10)

If you've never tasted creamy cheesecake topped with chocolate icing, you really owe yourself the favor. The chocolate icing is flavored with orange to blend more perfectly with the rich smoothness of the cheese filling that nestles under it. Perfect party fare.

CRUST
Ingredients

1¼ Cups chocolate wafer cookie crumbs
⅛ Teaspoon cinnamon
1 Tablespoon granulated sugar
5 Tablespoons butter

Directions

Measure cookie crumbs into mixing bowl. Add cinnamon and sugar. Stir. Melt butter. Mix with crumbs. Press over the bottom of a 9-inch spring-form pan. Bake for 5 minutes in an oven preheated to 300 degrees F.

CHEESE FILLING
Ingredients

2 Eight-ounce packages cream cheese, room temperature
½ Cup granulated sugar
¼ Teaspoon orange extract
2-Inch piece of vanilla bean (or ½ teaspoon vanilla)
2 Eggs, separated

Directions

Use the large mixing bowl of your mixer. Beat the cheese until it is light and puffy. Add sugar and orange extract. Split the vanilla bean and scrape out the soft inside. Add this to the sugar-cheese mixture and beat thoroughly. Add the egg yolks, one at a time, beating after each addition. Beat the egg whites until they are stiff. Fold them into the cheese mixture. Pour onto cooled crumb crust. Bake for 1 hour in an oven preheated to 300 degrees F.

TOPPING

Ingredients

1 Cup sour cream
1 Tablespoon granulated sugar
4-Inch piece of vanilla bean (or 1 teaspoon vanilla)

Directions

Mix the sour cream and the sugar together. Scrape the soft center from the vanilla bean. Add this to the sour cream mixture. Mix well. Spread this topping over the top of the hot cheesecake. Bake the cake for 10 minutes more at 300 degrees. Remove from the oven and cool thoroughly.

ICING

Ingredients

3 One-ounce squares semi-sweet chocolate
2 Tablespoons water
¼ Teaspoon orange extract
2 Tablespoons granulated sugar
2 Egg yolks
¼ Cup butter

Directions

Place the chocolate, the water, the orange extract, and the sugar in the top of a double boiler over boiling water and heat until the chocolate melts. Stir occasionally. Add the egg yolks, one at a time, beating after each addition. Cook over boiling water, stirring constantly for about 3 minutes. Allow to cool for 5 minutes. Beat in the butter, a bit at a time. Spread over the cooled cheesecake, reserving a small amount. Mix two or three drops of water with this remaining frosting. Dribble this from the top down over the sides of the cake. Chill slightly.

pumpkin
nut
ring

(Serves 8)

Here's a nutty ring, flavored with pumpkin, and iced with a zesty orange glaze.

CAKE
Ingredients

2⅓ Cups all-purpose flour
2 Teaspoons baking powder
1 Teaspoon baking soda
½ Teaspoon nutmeg
½ Teaspoon cinnamon

½ Teaspoon allspice
¼ Teaspoon cloves
½ Cup butter
1½ Cups granulated sugar
2 Eggs
½ Teaspoon vanilla extract
½ Cup canned pumpkin
¼ Cup mashed banana
Zest (orange-colored outside skin) of one small orange
½ Cup milk
½ Teaspoon lemon juice
½ Cup chopped pecans

Directions

Sift the flour, the baking powder, the baking soda, and the spices together. Cream the butter and the sugar. Beat in the eggs, one at a time, beating after each addition, and continuing to beat until the mixture is fluffy. Stir in the vanilla extract, the pumpkin, and the mashed banana. Carefully grate the thin orange outside layer of skin from one small orange, being sure not to include any of the bitter white underskin. Stir this orange zest into the batter. Measure the milk, add the lemon juice to it, and place this in a warm place until the milk curdles. Add the soured milk alternately with the sifted dry ingredients, mixing until smooth after each addition. Grease and flour a fluted tube pan and sprinkle in the chopped nuts. Carefully spoon the batter over the nuts and bake the cake in an oven preheated to 350 degrees F. The cake is done when it springs back when pressed lightly with the finger (about 35 to 40 minutes). Cool the cake on a rack and turn it onto a cake plate. Ice with Orange Glaze.

ORANGE GLAZE
Ingredients

1 Cup confectioners' sugar
¼ Cup orange juice

1 Egg white
10 Pecan halves

Directions

Mix the sugar and the orange juice until smooth. Beat the egg white until it is frothy and add to the sugar mixture. Beat at high speed for several minutes. Ice the top of the cooled cake, allowing the icing to drip over the edges and run down the sides of the cake. Arrange the pecan halves around the top of the cake.

fruit and nut bread

(Makes 1 loaf—serves 8)

Tea time calls for a sweet of its own. What could be more tempting than buttered fruit and nut bread?

Ingredients

1 Cup honey
1 Cup milk
½ Cup granulated sugar
5 Tablespoons butter
2 Egg yolks
2½ Cups all-purpose flour
1 Teaspoon baking soda
1 Teaspoon salt
1 Teaspoon powdered cinnamon
1 Teaspoon powdered anise
1 Cup coarsely chopped walnuts
½ Cup coarsely chopped dates
½ Cup coarsely chopped dried apricots

Directions

Stir the honey, the milk, and the sugar over a medium flame until the sugar is completely dissolved. Cool for 10 minutes and beat in the butter. Cool 10 minutes more and beat in the egg yolks. Sift together the flour, the soda, the salt, the cinnamon and the anise. Sift the dry ingredients into the batter and mix thoroughly. Soak the dried apricots in hot water for 5 minutes. Drain thoroughly. Chop the nuts, the dates, and the apricots and fold them into the batter. Butter and flour a bread pan and pour in the batter. Bake for 1¼ hours in an oven preheated to 325 degrees F. Leave the bread in the pan for 15 minutes and then turn out onto a rack and cool. Thinly slice and serve with sweet butter or cream cheese.

banana
pumpkin
spice cake

(Serves 8)

This is a dainty dish indeed, to set before a ladies' luncheon or a special bruncheon. It is as moist and tender a spice cake as you're ever likely to eat.

Ingredients

⅓ Cup shortening
1 Cup granulated sugar
1 Egg
2 Cups all-purpose flour
2 Teaspoons baking powder
½ Teaspoon baking soda
1 Teaspoon cinnamon
¼ Teaspoon allspice
¼ Teaspoon nutmeg

¼ Teaspoon salt
¼ Cup milk
¼ Teaspoon lemon juice
½ Cup cooked pumpkin
½ Cup very ripe bananas, mashed
¾ Cup chopped dates
¾ Cup peach jam
1 Cup finely chopped walnuts

Directions

Beat the shortening until it is smooth and soft. Gradually add the sugar, mixing thoroughly after each addition. When all the sugar has been added, cream the mixture until it is very smooth. Add the egg and beat thoroughly. Sift together the flour, the baking powder, the baking soda, the cinnamon, the allspice, the nutmeg, and the salt. Mix the milk and the lemon juice and put in a warm place to sour. Mix the pumpkin and the mashed banana, and stir in the sour milk. Stir the dry ingredients into the egg mixture alternately with the pumpkin mixture. Stir in the walnuts and the dates. Pour the batter into a well-oiled 9-inch tube pan and bake for one hour in an oven preheated to 350 degrees F. or until the cake tests done. Let the cake stand for about 15 minutes and remove it from the pan. When the cake is cool, spread it with the jam. Press the chopped walnuts over the cake.

banana bread with apricot topping

(Serves 8)

The ideal "something special" to serve with tea is this banana bread with tangy apricot topping.

TOPPING
  Ingredients

¾ Cup small dried apricots
¼ Cup granulated sugar
½ Cup boiling water

¼ Cup Grand Marnier
½ Cup apricot preserves

Directions

Soak the apricots in boiling water for ten minutes. Pour off the water. Place the apricots, the sugar, the ½ cup of boiling water, the Grand Marnier, and the apricot preserves in a saucepan and boil at medium-low heat until the apricots are barely covered in a thick syrup. Turn into a greased bundt pan (a round fluted mold with a tube in the center). Spread the apricots evenly in the bottom of the pan.

BANANA BREAD
Ingredients

2 Cups all-purpose flour
1½ Teaspoons baking powder
½ Teaspoon baking soda
¼ Teaspoon salt
¾ Cup coarsely chopped apricots
¾ Cup coarsely chopped dates
¾ Cup coarsely chopped nuts
1 Cup mashed ripe banana (about 3 medium-sized bananas)
2 Eggs
1 Cup granulated sugar
½ Cup butter
1½ Tablespoons milk
1 Teaspoon lemon juice

Directions

Sift together the flour, the baking powder, the baking soda, and the salt. Chop the apricots, the dates, and the nuts, and set aside. Place the mashed banana in a bowl, and add two lightly beaten eggs, the sugar, and the butter. Stir the lemon juice into the milk, add this to the banana mixture, and then beat until the mixture is smooth. Stir in the flour mixture thoroughly, and add the chopped apricots, the dates, and the nuts. Stir. Pour the batter over the apricots in the bundt pan. Place ¼ inch of water in an ovenproof baking dish and set in the cake pan. Bake in an oven preheated to 350 degrees F. for 1 hour, or until a toothpick tester comes out dry. While the cake is still in the pan, slice a piece from the top so that it will set evenly when it is inverted. Loosen around the outer edges and the center tube, and invert the cake onto a plate. Serve warm or at room temperature, with or without sweet butter.

fudge
brownie
pie

(Serves 8)

Here's a pie that's as rich and chewy, as flaky and crunchy, and as tempting a dessert as ever delighted an adult or child. You'd be wise to try it the very next time you find yourself in need of a company or a family treat.

CRUST

Ingredients

1 Cup all-purpose flour
½ Teaspoon salt
6 Tablespoons vegetable shortening
3 or 4 Tablespoons ice water

Directions

Sift the flour and salt into a mixing bowl. Cut in the shortening with a pastry blender or two knives until the particles are the size of small peas. Sprinkle in the ice water and stir with a fork until the pastry forms a ball. Let the mixture stand for 15 minutes. Roll out the pastry on a lightly floured surface. Fit a circle of dough into a 9-inch pie plate. Do not stretch the dough. Crimp the edges of the pie shell.

FILLING

Ingredients

1 Cup butter
2 Cups granulated sugar
2 Teaspoons vanilla
4 Eggs
2 Squares unsweetened chocolate
2 Squares semi-sweet chocolate
⅔ Cup sifted all-purpose flour
¼ Teaspoon salt
¾ Cup shelled walnut pieces

Directions

Cream the butter until it is light and fluffy. Add the sugar gradually. Cream the butter and sugar until puffy and light in color. Add the vanilla. Stir well. Add the egg yolks, one at a time, beating well after each addition. Melt the chocolate in the top of a double boiler over boiling water. Sift the flour again and add the flour and the chocolate to the butter-sugar mixture. Mix well. Beat the egg whites with the salt until they are stiff, but not dry. Fold these and the walnut pieces gently into the chocolate mixture. Turn the filling into the unbaked pie shell and bake in an oven preheated to 350 degrees F. for 45 minutes or until the pie is puffy across the top. Remove from the oven and cool thoroughly.

TOPPING

Ingredients

1 Cup heavy cream
3 Tablespoons granulated sugar
8 Walnut halves
A sprinkling of grated semi-sweet chocolate

Directions

Whip the cream until it forms a soft peak. Gradually add the sugar and beat until fairly stiff. Use a pastry tube fitted with a fluted nozzle to pipe the cream onto the top of the cooled pie. Place the walnut halves at regular intervals around the outside edge of the pie. Sprinkle with the grated chocolate. Serve immediately.

treacle
pie

(Serves 8)

*The miraculous filling for this rich pie separates itself
into two marvelous textures—one creamy, one syrupy—
both scrumptious.*

PECAN CRUST
Ingredients

1 Ounce unsweetened chocolate
¾ Cup all-purpose flour
5 Tablespoons brown sugar
½ Teaspoon salt
⅓ Cup cold butter
½ Cup coarsely chopped pecans
1 Tablespoon cold water
1 Teaspoon vanilla extract

Directions

Grate the chocolate and chill it until needed. Sift together the flour, the sugar, and the salt. Cut the butter into small pieces and add it along with the chopped pecans and grated chocolate to the dry ingredients. Work with the fingers until the mixture is thoroughly blended. Sprinkle the water and the vanilla extract over the chocolate-nut mixture and stir with a fork until the crust holds together. Roll out between two sheets of waxed paper and fit into a 9-inch glass pie plate. Bake in an oven preheated to 350 degrees F. until the crust is brown. Cool the pie shell in the dish.

TREACLE FILLING
Ingredients

1¼ Cups confectioners' sugar
¾ Cup butter
3 Eggs
2 Ounces unsweetened chocolate
2 Teaspoons dry instant coffee

Directions

Sift the sugar and cream it with the butter until the mixture is smooth and fluffy. Add the eggs, one at a time, and mix slowly for several minutes after each addition. Melt the chocolate in the top of a double boiler, cool it slightly, and stir it, with the dry instant coffee, into the sugar-butter mixture. Turn the filling into the cooled pie shell and chill for 1 hour.

TOPPING
Ingredients

1 Cup heavy cream
3 Tablespoons granulated sugar
1 Tablespoon crème de cacao
18 Pecan halves
A sprinkling of grated semi-sweet chocolate

Directions

Beat the cream until it begins to thicken. Continue beating while you sprinkle in the sugar. Beat until the cream holds a peak. Stir in the crème de cacao. Pipe the cream in swirls over the top of the pie. Sprinkle with the grated chocolate and arrange the pecan halves around the edge. Serve very cold.

minted
black
bottom
pie

(Serves 8)

Looking for a frosty dessert to serve on a sweltering day? Among the coolest is this rum-flavored, two-tone mint pie.

CRUST
Ingredients

1¼ Cups thin chocolate wafer cookies crushed to fine crumbs
⅛ Teaspoon cinnamon
1 Tablespoon granulated sugar
5 Tablespoons butter

Directions

Measure cookie crumbs into mixing bowl. Add cinnamon and sugar. Stir. Melt butter and mix with the crumbs. Press over the bottom of a 9-inch pie plate. Bake for 5 minutes in an oven preheated to 300 degrees F.

FILLING
Ingredients

½ Cup granulated sugar
1¼ Tablespoons cornstarch
4 Egg yolks
2 Cups milk
1¼ Tablespoons unflavored gelatin
¼ Cup water
1 Square unsweetened chocolate
¼ Teaspoon mint extract
1 Square semi-sweet chocolate
½ Teaspoon vanilla
4 Egg whites
¼ Teaspoon cream of tartar
½ Cup granulated sugar
2 Tablespoons dark rum
½ Cup whipped cream
2 Thin solid chocolate after-dinner mints
16 Fresh mint leaves (if desired)

Directions

Mix ½ cup of sugar and the cornstarch in the top of a double boiler. Add the egg yolks and mix thoroughly. Scald the milk and stir it into the egg yolk mixture. Cook over boiling water, stirring, until the custard is thick enough to coat a spoon. Sprinkle the gelatin over the ¼ cup of water to soften. Stir the softened gelatin into the hot custard and continue to stir until the gelatin is completely dissolved. Divide the custard in half.

Place the chocolate in the top of a double boiler. Melt over boiling water. Cool the chocolate and stir in the vanilla. Add the melted chocolate and the mint extract to one-half of the custard. Mix thoroughly and pour into the cooled pie shell. Chill until firm.

Beat the egg whites with the cream of tartar until they are stiff enough to stand in peaks when you lift the beater. Add ½ cup of sugar slowly, beating steadily and continuing to beat the meringue until it holds its shape. Add the rum to the cooled vanilla custard. Fold in the meringue. Spread this custard over the chilled chocolate filling. Chill thoroughly. Decorate the pie by piping a ribbon of whipped cream around the edge with a pastry tube. Break the thin mints into quarters and place at regular intervals around the pie. Tuck a fresh mint leaf on either side of each mint quarter. Serve very cold.

frozen
lime
pie

(Serves 8)

Prepare this frosty pie a day or two before your next dinner party and store it in your freezer. When dessert time rolls around, merely top with sweetened whipped cream and serve. It's a really cool dessert for a sizzling summer day.

CRUST
Ingredients

1¾ Cups graham cracker crumbs
8 Tablespoons butter
¼ Cup granulated sugar
1 Teaspoon cinnamon

Directions

Place the cracker crumbs in a bowl. Melt the butter and sprinkle it over the crumbs. Add the sugar and the cinnamon and mix thoroughly. Press the crumb mixture against the bottom and sides of a 9-inch pie dish. Bake for 15 minutes in an oven preheated to 375 degrees F. Cool the crust in the dish.

FILLING
Ingredients

5 Egg yolks
1 Can sweetened condensed milk
¼ Cup granulated sugar
1 Cup fresh lime juice

Directions

Beat the egg yolks until they are lemon colored. Gradually beat in the condensed milk, the sugar, and the lime juice. Pour this into the pie crust and freeze.

TO SERVE THE PIE
Ingredients

1 Cup heavy cream
3 Tablespoons granulated sugar

Directions

When ready to serve the pie, whip the cream until it begins to thicken. Beat in the sugar and continue to beat until the cream is fairly stiff. Remove the pie from the freezer, top with the whipped cream, and serve immediately.

lime
meringue
pie

(Serves 8)

If lemon meringue pie is one of your favorite desserts, you should by all means try this equally tart, equally delicious, and far more exotic lime dessert.

CRUST
Ingredients

1 Cup all-purpose flour
½ Teaspoon salt
6 Tablespoons vegetable shortening
3 or 4 Tablespoons ice water

Directions

Sift the flour and the salt into a mixing bowl. Cut in the shortening with a pastry blender or two knives until the particles are the size of small peas. Sprinkle in the ice water and stir with a fork until the pastry forms a ball. Let stand 15 minutes. Roll out the pastry on a lightly floured surface. Fit the circle of dough into a 9-inch pie plate. Do not stretch the dough. Crimp the edges of the pie shell and prick the bottom with a fork. Bake at 450 degrees F.

for 10 to 15 minutes or until golden brown. Remove from the oven and allow to cool.

FILLING
Ingredients

1 Cup granulated sugar
½ Cup all-purpose flour
¼ Teaspoon salt
3 Tablespoons cornstarch
2 Cups water
4 Egg yolks
¼ Cup lime juice
Grated rind of one lemon
1 Tablespoon butter
3 or 4 Drops green coloring

Directions

Mix the sugar, flour, salt, cornstarch, and ½ cup of water in the top of a double boiler. Add the remaining water and stir until smooth. Cook over medium heat until the mixture is thick and smooth. Stir this hot mixture into the beaten egg yolks and continue cooking over hot water for 4 or 5 minutes. Do not allow to boil. Stir in the lime juice, the lemon rind, the butter, and the green coloring. Allow to cool slightly.

MERINGUE
Ingredients

5 Egg whites
¼ Teaspoon cream of tartar
10 Tablespoons granulated sugar
1 Tablespoon grated coconut

Directions

Beat the egg whites until they are light and frothy. Add the cream of tartar. Beat again until the egg whites are stiff and hold a peak. Add the sugar a little at a time, beating after each addition until the meringue is stiff and glossy. Pour the cooled lime filling into the cooled pie shell. Heap the meringue onto the pie filling. Spread it until it touches the sides of the pie shell. Use a spoon to swirl the meringue into peaks. Sprinkle with the coconut. Bake in an oven preheated to 425 degrees F. for 5 to 6 minutes, or until the top is attractively browned. Allow to cool at room temperature. Chill in the refrigerator for several hours before serving.

pecan
pie

(Serves 8)

My Kentucky-born great-Aunt Katherine Scheperd gave me this recipe for pecan pie filling. It is an updated version of a recipe she received from an acquaintance who resided in Mobile, Alabama, during the Civil War. I pass it on to you. Hope you enjoy it as much as we do.

CRUST
Ingredients

1 Cup all-purpose flour
½ Teaspoon salt
6 Tablespoons vegetable shortening
3 or 4 Tablespoons ice water

Directions

Sift the flour and the salt into a mixing bowl. Cut in the shortening with a pastry blender or two knives, until the particles are the size of small peas. Sprinkle in the ice water and stir with a fork until the pastry forms a ball. Let stand for 15 minutes. Roll out the pastry on a lightly floured surface. Fit the circle of dough into a 9-inch pie plate. Do not stretch the dough. Crimp the edges of the pie shell.

FILLING
Ingredients

2½ Tablespoons granulated sugar
2 Cups corn syrup
4 Tablespoons all-purpose flour
5 Eggs
¾ Teaspoon salt
1¼ Teaspoons vanilla
2 Tablespoons melted butter
¾ Cup chopped pecans

Directions

Place the sugar, the corn syrup, and the flour in a bowl and mix thoroughly. Beat the eggs, add to the corn syrup mixture, and beat well. Add the salt, the vanilla, and the melted butter, and beat again. Pour the filling into the unbaked pastry shell. Sprinkle the chopped nuts evenly over the top of the filling. Place the pie in an oven preheated to 375 degrees F. Immediately turn the heat to 350 degrees F. and bake for 40 to 45 minutes or until the center is set, but not firm. Cool the pie to room temperature and then chill. Serve with sweetened whipped cream flavored with Crème de Cacao.

macadamia pie

Would you believe that any nut pie could taste more rich or smooth, more divinely "nutty" than pecan pie? It is possible. For proof, try this macadamia nut delight. Costly, but worth it for a special occasion.

CRUST

Ingredients

1½ Cups all-purpose flour
¾ Teaspoon salt

9 Tablespoons shortening
4 to 6 Tablespoons ice water

Directions

Sift the flour and the salt into a mixing bowl. Cut in the shortening with a pastry blender or two knives, until the particles are the size of small peas. Sprinkle in 4 tablespoons of ice water while tossing with a fork. If the dough is not moist enough to form a ball, sprinkle in another tablespoon of ice water. Toss again. If necessary, add another tablespoon of water. Do not add too much water, or the dough will become sticky. Chill for 20 minutes. Roll the pastry, from the center out, on a floured surface to a circle 11½ inches by ⅛ inch thick, and fit it into a 9-inch ovenproof glass pie plate. Do not stretch the dough. Flute the edges with the fingers.

FILLING

Ingredients

4 Eggs
1⅓ Cups light corn syrup
1 Cup granulated sugar
4 Tablespoons light rum

2 Cups chopped, salted macadamia nuts
3 Tablespoons melted butter
1½ Teaspoons vanilla

Directions

Beat together the eggs, the corn syrup, the sugar, and the rum. Chop the nuts and stir them into the egg-syrup mixture, along with the melted butter and the vanilla extract. Mix well. Pour the filling into the unbaked pie shell, and bake the pie in an oven preheated to 325 degrees F. for 60 minutes or until the filling is set. Cool the pie and then chill it. Serve with whipped cream.

apple-marron pie

Apple pie in company dress is this rich apple treat studded with marron and pecan halves, and topped with whipped cream.

CRUST
Ingredients

2 Cups all-purpose flour
1 Teaspoon salt

12 Tablespoons vegetable shortening
6 to 8 Tablespoons ice water

Directions

Sift the flour and the salt into a mixing bowl. Cut in the shortening with a pastry blender or two knives, until the particles are the size of small peas. Sprinkle in the ice water and stir with a fork until the pastry forms a ball. Let stand for 15 minutes. Roll out half the pastry on a lightly floured surface. Fit the circle of dough into a 9-inch pie plate. Do not stretch the dough. Crimp the edges of the pie shell.

FILLING
Ingredients

8 Medium-sized pippin apples,
  peeled, quartered, and cored
3 Tablespoons granulated sugar
1 Teaspoon nutmeg
1 Teaspoon cinnamon

½ Cup of the vanilla syrup
  that covers the marrons
1 10-Ounce jar marrons
20 Pecan halves

Directions

Place the peeled and cored apple quarters in a saucepan with the sugar, the nutmeg, the cinnamon, and the vanilla syrup. Cook over *low* heat for 8 minutes. Cool to room temperature, stir in the whole marrons and the pecan halves, and turn the mixture into the unbaked pie shell. Cover with a top crust, pierced for the escape of steam. Bake for 10 minutes in an oven preheated to 450 degrees F., and then reduce the heat to 350 degrees F. and bake for 30 minutes more. Serve warm, topped with whipped cream.

apple pie with english custard

(Serves 8)

Are you in need of a dessert suggestion for a family get-together? Why not bake a spicy apple pie and serve it hot with a choice of ice cream or smooth English custard as a topping?

CRUST

Ingredients

2 Cups all-purpose flour
1 Teaspoon salt
12 Tablespoons vegetable shortening
6 to 8 Tablespoons ice water

Directions

Sift the flour and the salt into a mixing bowl. Cut in the shortening with a pastry blender or two knives, until the particles are the size of small peas. Sprinkle in the ice water and stir with a fork until the pastry forms a ball. Chill the mixture for 15 minutes. Roll out the pastry on a lightly floured surface. Fit a circle of dough into a 9-inch plate. Do not stretch the dough.

FILLING
Ingredients

8 Medium-sized pippin apples	Pinch of ginger
¾ Cup granulated sugar	1 Tablespoon fresh lemon juice
1 Teaspoon ground nutmeg	3 Tablespoons granulated sugar
1 Teaspoon ground cinnamon	3 Tablespoons butter
⅛ Teaspoon mace	

Directions

Peel and core the apples and cut them into eighths. Combine the apples, the sugar, and the spices in a saucepan and stir over a low flame for 5 minutes. Cool. Spoon the filling into the unbaked pie shell. Sprinkle with lemon juice and 3 tablespoons of sugar. Dot with butter. Roll out the remaining pastry dough and fit over the pie. Crimp the edges and cut 8 small slits in the top. Bake for 15 minutes in an oven preheated to 450 degrees F. Reduce oven heat to 375 degrees F. and bake for 30 minutes. Remove the pie from the oven, brush the top (not the edges) with cream or beaten egg. Sprinkle with granulated sugar, return to the oven, and bake for 10 minutes more. Serve hot with ice cream or English custard.

ENGLISH CUSTARD
Ingredients

4 Eggs
½ Cup granulated sugar
1 Cup milk
½ Cup heavy cream
2-Inch piece of vanilla bean (or ½ teaspoon vanilla extract)

Directions

Beat the eggs in the top of a double boiler. Add the sugar and continue beating until thoroughly mixed. Scald the milk with the heavy cream and the split vanilla bean. (If vanilla extract is used, it must be added after the custard is cooled.) Pour the scalded milk mixture gradually into the eggs, stirring constantly. Place over simmering water and stir until the mixture thickens slightly. Do not overcook or the custard will curdle. Strain the custard and serve it hot or cold in a separate dish along with the pie.

blueberry
pie

(Serves 8)

Especially rich and creamy is this blueberry pie made with sour cream.

CRUST

Ingredients

1 Cup all-purpose flour
½ Teaspoon salt
6 Tablespoons vegetable shortening
3 or 4 Tablespoons ice water

Directions

Sift the flour and the salt into a mixing bowl. Cut in the shortening with a pastry blender or two knives until particles are the size of small peas. Sprinkle in the ice water and stir with a fork until the pastry forms a ball. Let stand for 15 minutes. Roll out the pastry on a lightly floured surface. Fit a circle of dough into a 9-inch pie plate. Do not stretch the dough. Crimp the edges of the pie shell.

FILLING

Ingredients

1 Cup granulated sugar
3 Tablespoons all-purpose flour
1⅓ Cups sour cream
1 Egg

¾ Teaspoon vanilla extract
¼ Teaspoon salt
2½ Cups blueberries

Directions

Mix the sugar and the flour. Beat in the sour cream, the egg, the vanilla, and the salt. Mix until smooth. Wash and dry the blueberries and remove any stems. Fold the blueberries into the sour cream mixture, turn them into the unbaked pie shell, and bake for 35 minutes in an oven preheated to 450 degrees F.

TOPPING

Ingredients

¾ Cup granulated sugar
9 Tablespoons all-purpose flour
1½ Teaspoons cinnamon
6 Tablespoons butter

Directions

Mix the sugar, the flour, and the cinnamon. Cut in the butter until the mixture resembles coarse crumbs. Sprinkle this over the pie and bake for 10 to 15 minutes more. Cool.

banana coconut cream pie

(Serves 8)

This is a coconut cream pie with a double surprise! The rich, yellow, coconut cream filling is topped with sliced bananas and a high, fluffy meringue. Your family will love this delicate pie as much as will your dinner guests.

CRUST

Ingredients

1 Cup all-purpose flour
½ Teaspoon salt
6 Tablespoons vegetable shortening
3 or 4 Tablespoons ice water

Directions

Sift the flour and the salt into a mixing bowl. Cut in the shortening with a pastry blender or two knives until the particles are the size of small peas. Sprinkle in the ice water and stir with a fork until the pastry forms a ball. Let the mixture stand 15 minutes. Roll out the pastry on a lightly floured surface. Fit into a 9-inch pie plate. Do not stretch the dough. Crimp the edges of the pie shell and prick the bottom with a fork. Bake at 450 degrees F.

for 10 to 15 minutes or until golden. Remove from the oven and allow to cool.

FILLING
Ingredients

⅓ Cup all-purpose flour
⅓ Teaspoon salt
5 Tablespoons granulated sugar
2 Cups milk
4 Egg yolks
1 Cup grated fresh coconut
1 Teaspoon each vanilla and almond extract
1 Banana

Directions

Sift the flour into the top of a double boiler. Add the salt, the sugar, and ½ cup of milk. Stir. Add 1½ cups hot milk, stirring constantly. Cook over hot water until mixture thickens, while continuing to stir. Beat the egg yolks until they are lemon colored. Pour a little of the mixture from the pan into the egg yolks. Blend. Return egg mixture to pan. Add grated coconut and continue cooking and stirring for 3 or 4 minutes. Stir this filling over cracked ice until it is fairly cool. Add the vanilla and the almond flavorings. Mix well. Slice banana and place on filling.

MERINGUE
Ingredients

5 Egg whites
¼ Teaspoon cream of tartar
10 Tablespoons granulated sugar

Directions

Beat the egg whites until they are light and frothy. Add the cream of tartar. Beat again until the egg whites are stiff and hold a peak. Add the sugar a little at a time, beating after each addition until the meringue is stiff and glossy. Pour the cooled coconut filling into the pie shell. Heap the meringue on the pie filling. Spread it until it touches the sides of the pie shell. Use a spoon to swirl the meringue into peaks. Bake in an oven preheated to 425 degrees F. for 5 or 6 minutes, or until the top is attractively browned. Allow to cool at room temperature. Chill in the refrigerator for several hours before serving.

apricot
pie

Apricot nectar and rose water flavor this apricot-topped pie.

CRUST
Ingredients

1½ Cups all-purpose flour
¾ Teaspoon salt
9 Tablespoons shortening
4 to 6 Tablespoons ice water

Directions

Sift together the flour and the salt. In a mixing bowl, cut in the shortening with a pastry blender or two knives until the particles are the size of small peas. Sprinkle in 4 tablespoons of ice water while tossing with a fork. If the dough is not moist enough to form a ball, sprinkle in another tablespoon of ice water. Toss again. If necessary, add another tablespoon of water. Do not add too much water or the dough will become sticky. Chill the mixture for 20 minutes. Roll the pastry, from the center out, on a floured surface, to a circle 11½ inches by ⅛ inch thick, and fit it into a 9-inch ovenproof glass pie plate. Do not stretch the dough. Flute the edges with the fingers, and with a fork prick the bottom and the sides. Bake for 15 minutes in an oven preheated to 450 degrees F. Cool the shell.

FILLING
Ingredients

2 Eggs
6 Apricot halves, very fancy canned
1½ Cups apricot nectar
¼ Teaspoon salt
½ Cup granulated sugar

1 Tablespoon unflavored gelatin
2 Teaspoons lemon juice
½ Teaspoon rose water
½ Cup heavy cream

Directions

Separate the egg yolks from the whites. Beat the egg yolks lightly. Rub the apricots through a sieve. Mix the egg yolks, the strained apricots, the apricot nectar, the salt, and ¼ cup of sugar in the top of a double boiler. Cook the mixture over hot water until it thickens slightly, stirring constantly. Soften the gelatin in the lemon juice and rose water. Add this to the hot apricot custard and stir until the gelatin is dissolved. Fill the bottom of the double boiler with cold water. Place the top of the double boiler over the cold water and allow the mixture to cool until it is slightly thickened. Beat the egg whites until they are stiff. Add the remaining sugar, 2 tablespoons at a time, beating after each addition. Continue to beat until the meringue stands in very stiff peaks.

Fold the meringue into the apricot mixture. Whip the cream and fold this in also. Pour the apricot cream filling into the pastry shell and chill for several hours or until firm.

TOPPING
Ingredients

16 Apricot halves, very fancy canned
½ Cup apricot jam or preserves
1 Teaspoon rose water
¼ Cup blanched almonds, slivered
¼ Cup sour cream (or sweetened whipped heavy cream)

Directions

Place the apricot halves on a double thickness of paper toweling to drain. Heat the apricot jam and the rose water. Pat the apricot halves dry and place them attractively, with round side up, over the pie. Cover the apricots with jam. Sprinkle the almond slivers carefully *between* the apricot halves. Place the sour cream in a pastry bag and pipe tiny points between the apricot halves and around the outside of the pie. Serve very cold.

strawberry
mint
julep
pie

(Serves 8)

Cool and colorful is this frothy pink pie with chocolate mint crust.

CRUST
Ingredients

1 Cup filberts (hazelnuts)
2 One-ounce squares semi-sweet chocolate
2 Tablespoons heavy cream
½ Cup macaroon crumbs
5 Drops mint flavoring

Directions

Reduce the nuts to a coarse powder in a blender or grinder. Melt the chocolate in the top of a double boiler. Add the heavy cream. Stir. Measure the macaroon crumbs into a small mixing bowl. Add the ground nuts, the melted chocolate, and the mint flavoring. Mix thoroughly. Lightly grease the bottom of an ovenproof glass pie plate. Press the chocolate-nut mixture firmly and evenly against the sides and bottom of a pie plate. Place in the freezer or refrigerator while preparing the filling.

FILLING
Ingredients

2 Cups frozen strawberries with their syrup
4 Tablespoons water
2 Tablespoons unflavored gelatin
1 Cup heavy cream

Directions

Place the thawed strawberries and strawberry syrup in the blender, reserving ½ cup strawberry syrup. Blend the strawberries for 25 seconds at low speed (or crush berries with a spoon). Place water in a cup or small bowl. Sprinkle gelatin over water to soften. Heat the reserved ½ cup of strawberry liquid, add the softened gelatin to this, and stir until the gelatin is dissolved. Stir the gelatin mixture into the blended strawberry liquid. Cool the mixture until it begins to thicken. Whip the heavy cream and gently fold it into the slightly thickened strawberry mixture. Spoon this into the cooled pie shell. Chill the pie until the filling is firm.

TOPPING
Ingredients

1 Cup heavy cream
3 Tablespoons sugar

Directions

Whip the heavy cream until it forms a soft peak. Gradually add the sugar and whip the cream until it is fairly stiff. Top the pie filling with the whipped cream.

Decorate the top of the pie with 8 whole strawberries and 16 fresh mint leaves. Serve very cold.

strawberry
pie

(Serves 8)

Here, large, fresh strawberries and chilled vanilla cream nestle together in a flaky pie crust under a decorative cover of swirled almond-flavored whipped cream.

CRUST
Ingredients

1½ Cups all-purpose flour
¾ Teaspoon salt
9 Tablespoons shortening
4 to 6 Tablespoons ice water

Directions

Sift together the flour and the salt. In a mixing bowl, cut in the shortening with a pastry blender or two knives until the particles are the size of small peas. Sprinkle in 4 tablespoons of ice water while tossing with a fork. If the dough is not moist enough to form a ball, sprinkle in another tablespoon of ice water. Toss again. If necessary, add another tablespoon of water. Do not add too much water or the dough will become sticky. Chill for 20 minutes. Roll the pastry, from the center out, on a floured surface to a circle 11½ inches by ⅛ inch and fit it into a 9-inch Pyrex pie plate. Do not stretch the dough. Flute the edges with the fingers and, with a fork, prick the bottom and the sides. Bake for 15 minutes in an oven preheated to 450 degrees F. Cool the shell.

VANILLA CREAM
Ingredients

⅓ Cup plus 1 tablespoon granulated sugar
2 Tablespoons cornstarch
6 Egg yolks
1½ Cups milk
½ Cup heavy cream

3-Inch piece of vanilla bean (or 1½ teaspoons vanilla extract)
1½ Tablespoons unflavored gelatin
3 Tablespoons cold water
6 Tablespoons *whipped** cream

Directions

Place the sugar, the cornstarch, and the egg yolks in the top of a double boiler. Mix well. Use another saucepan to scald the milk and the heavy cream. Slit the vanilla bean and stir it into the milk. (If vanilla extract is used, it must be added after the vanilla cream is chilled.) Pour the scalded milk and cream, with the vanilla bean, slowly over the egg yolk mixture, stirring rapidly. Cook the mixture over boiling water, stirring continually until it is quite thick. Soften the gelatin in the cold water and stir it into the hot cream mixture until the gelatin has completely dissolved. Bring the cream to room temperature, remove the vanilla bean, and then chill *slightly*. Fold in the *whipped** cream.

TO ASSEMBLE THE PIE
Ingredients

¾ Cup strawberry jam or preserves
1½ Quarts *large,* whole, *ripe, fresh* strawberries
¾ Cup heavy cream
¼ Cup granulated sugar
5 Drops almond extract

Directions

Whip the cream with the sugar and almond extract. Brush the bottom of the cooled pie shell with strawberry jam, reserving about half to glaze the strawberries. Wash the berries, and carefully pinch off the stems. Dry the berries thoroughly and arrange them, stem side down, on the glazed pie shell. Brush the berries with the remaining jam and spoon the vanilla cream over them. Chill for 2 hours. When the pie has set, decorate the top with points of the whipped cream, piped through a fancy nozzle of a pastry bag. Serve cold.

* This pie is decorated with whipped cream as a final step. Whip the cream as instructed in "TO ASSEMBLE THE PIE" and use 6 tablespoons of this in the above.

orange-glazed almond cream pie

Imagine, if you will, a cool, smooth almond cream (with just a hint of texture) tucked into a pie crust and topped with a clear orange glaze. You have just conjured up a picture of this elegant pie.

CRUST

Ingredients

1½ Cups all-purpose flour
¾ Teaspoon salt

9 Tablespoons shortening
4 to 6 Tablespoons ice water

Directions

Sift the flour and the salt into a mixing bowl. Cut in the shortening with a pastry blender or two knives until the particles are the size of small peas. Sprinkle in 4 tablespoons of ice water while tossing with a fork. If the dough is not moist enough to form a ball, sprinkle in another tablespoon of ice water. Toss again. If necessary, add another tablespoon of water. Do not add too much water, or the dough will become sticky. Chill for 20 minutes. Roll the pastry, from the center out, on a floured surface, to a circle 11½ inches by ⅛ inch thick and fit it into a 9-inch ovenproof glass plate. Do not stretch the dough. Flute the edges with the fingers, and with a fork, prick the bottom and sides. Bake for 15 minutes in an oven preheated to 450 degrees F. Cool the shell.

FILLING

Ingredients

1 Cup almond paste
2 Cups milk
2 Tablespoons granulated sugar
4 Egg yolks

1½ Tablespoons unflavored gelatin
¼ Cup cold water
1 Cup heavy cream
½ Teaspoon almond extract

Directions

Place the almond paste and ¾ cup of milk in the container of a blender. Blend at low speed until the mixture is smooth. Pour the blended almond milk, the remaining milk, and the sugar into a saucepan and stir over a low flame until the mixture is hot and smooth. Beat the egg yolks in the top of a double boiler, until they are lemon colored. Pour the hot almond over the beaten egg yolks, a little at a time, and cook over boiling water, stirring constantly until the mixture thickens enough to cover the spoon. *Do not allow to boil.* Soften the gelatin in the water and stir it into the hot almond cream. Cool over cracked ice until the cream begins to set. Whip the heavy cream and fold it, together with the almond extract, into the almond cream. Turn the filling into the baked, cooled pie shell. Place the pie in the freezer for an hour or refrigerate for 3 hours before topping it with the orange sections and the Orange Glaze.

ORANGE GLAZE
Ingredients

1 Cup orange juice
1 Cup granulated sugar
1½ Tablespoons cornstarch
¼ Cup cold water

Directions

Bring the orange juice and the sugar to a boil. Mix the cornstarch and the water to a smooth paste and stir several spoonfuls of the hot orange syrup into it. Pour this mixture into the remaining hot orange syrup and boil over a medium flame for several minutes, stirring constantly until the glaze is thick and clear. Cool.

TO ASSEMBLE THE PIE
Ingredients

2 or 3 Fancy oranges
¼ Cup heavy cream

Directions

Peel the oranges and carefully cut the orange sections from the membranes. Drain these orange sections and arrange them attractively on the top of the chilled almond cream. Spread the cooled orange glaze over the orange sections. Place the pie in the freezer for ½ hour or refrigerate for 1½ hours before serving. When you are ready to serve the pie, whip the heavy cream and pipe it through a small nozzle of a pastry tube to form little rosettes near the base of each orange segment. Serve cold.

black
cherry
pie

(Serves 8)

If black cherries are your weakness, this pie is for you.

CRUST

Ingredients

1½ Cups all-purpose flour
¾ Teaspoon salt
9 Tablespoons shortening
4 to 6 Tablespoons ice water

Directions

Sift the flour and the salt into a mixing bowl. Cut in the shortening with a pastry blender or two knives until the particles are the size of small peas. Sprinkle in 4 tablespoons of ice water while tossing with a fork. If the dough is not moist enough to form a ball, sprinkle in another tablespoon of ice water. Toss again. If necessary, add another tablespoon of water. Do not add too much water or the dough will become sticky. Chill for 20 minutes. Roll out the pastry on a floured surface to a circle 9¼ inches across and fit it into the bottom of an assembled 9-inch spring-form pan. Prick with a fork and bake for 15 minutes in an oven preheated to 450 degrees F. Cool in the pan.

CUSTARD FILLING
Ingredients

2½ Cups milk
¼ Cup plus 1 tablespoon
  granulated sugar
1¼ Tablespoons all-purpose flour
4 Egg yolks
1 Tablespoon unflavored gelatin

2 Tablespoons water
1 Tablespoon Grand Marnier
½ Teaspoon vanilla extract
4 Egg whites

Directions

Heat the milk in the top of a double boiler. Mix the sugar and the flour, add the egg yolks, and mix well. Add the milk a little at a time and stir until smooth. Cook over simmering water, stirring constantly until it thickens enough to cover a spoon rather thickly. *Do not overcook.* Soften the gelatin in the water and Grand Marnier. Stir into the hot custard. Cool over ice water, stirring constantly. Stir in the vanilla. Beat the egg whites until they hold a stiff peak and fold them into the cooled custard. Pour into the cooled pastry shell and chill until firm.

CHERRY TOPPING
Ingredients

1 Large can pitted black cherries
½ Cup seedless raspberry jelly or jam
3 Tablespoons Cherry Marnier

Directions

Drain the cherries and place them in a saucepan with the strained raspberry jelly and the Cherry Marnier. Stir over low heat until the sauce is thick. Cool completely and spread gently over the firm custard. Chill.

WHIPPED CREAM

1 Cup heavy cream
3 Tablespoons granulated sugar

Directions

Beat the cream until it has thickened slightly but is not yet stiff. Continue beating while you sprinkle in the sugar. Beat until the cream holds a peak and pipe it in swirls over the top of the pie. Serve very cold.

frozen
marron
cream
pie

(Serves 8)

Marrons and whipped cream combine their smooth, rich flavors for a filling, and semi-sweet chocolate nestles up to hazelnuts and macaroon crumbs for the "crust" of this special company pie.

Ingredients

1 Cup filberts (hazelnuts)
2 One-ounce squares semi-sweet chocolate
2 Tablespoons heavy cream
½ Cup macaroon crumbs
2 Tablespoons Cointreau
4 Tablespoons water
2 Teaspoons unflavored gelatin
2 Ten-ounce jars of marrons in vanilla syrup
1 Pint heavy cream
Semi-sweet chocolate curls or grated chocolate for decoration

Directions

Place the large bowl of your electric mixer in the refrigerator or freezer. Reduce the nuts to a coarse powder in a blender or grinder. Melt 2 ounces of chocolate in the top of a double boiler. Add 2 tablespoons of heavy cream. Stir. Measure macaroon crumbs into a small mixing bowl. Add the ground nuts and the melted chocolate. Mix thoroughly. Lightly grease the bottom of a spring-form pan. Assemble the pan. Press the chocolate-nut mixture firmly and evenly into the bottom of the pan. Place in the freezer or refrigerator. Measure the Cointreau and 2 tablespoons of water into a very small saucepan or saucepan-type measuring cup. Simmer over a tiny flame until the liquid is reduced by half. Place the remaining 2 tablespoons of water in a small bowl or measuring cup. Sprinkle in the gelatin and stir until moist. Pour the hot Cointreau mixture into this and stir until the gelatin is dissolved. Mash the marrons and liquid from one jar until the marron pieces are the size of large peas. Stir together the marron and Cointreau mixture. Remove the large bowl from the refrigerator or freezer. Pour in 1 pint of heavy cream and beat until the cream is fairly stiff. Fold the whipped cream and the marron mixture together. Remove the spring-form pan from the freezer or refrigerator and spoon the marron cream over the chocolate "crust." Place the pie in the freezer for 3 hours. To serve, carefully run a sharp knife around the edge of the marron cream. Loosen the "crust" from the pan with a cake server. Carefully slide the pie onto the serving plate. Decorate the top of the pie with chocolate curls or grated chocolate. Place 8 whole marrons at regular intervals around the outside of the pie. Serve very cold.

baked
alaska*

(Serves 8 to 10)

This ice cream treat is sure to be a conversation piece at any meal.

SPONGE CAKE
  Ingredients

8 Egg yolks
¾ Cup granulated sugar
6 Tablespoons ground almonds
6 Tablespoons all-purpose flour
5 Egg whites
5 Drops almond extract
1 Lemon

* Prepare cake and ice cream mold a day in advance of serving.

Directions

Cream the egg yolks and the sugar until they are light and fluffy. Stir in the ground almonds and the flour. Beat the egg whites until they hold a stiff peak. Fold the beaten egg whites into the egg yolk-nut mixture. Squeeze and strain the juice of the lemon. Add the almond extract and the lemon juice to the batter and mix gently, but well. Place the batter in a buttered 9½- x 12½-inch cake pan and bake for 25 to 30 minutes in an oven preheated to 350 degrees F., until the center of the cake springs back when lightly pressed with the finger. Cool in the pan.

TO ASSEMBLE THE DESSERT
Ingredients

1 10-Ounce jar marrons glacés in vanilla syrup
1 Pint pistachio ice cream
1 Pint chocolate ice cream
1 Quart peach ice cream
7 Egg whites
1 ⅔ Cups confectioners' sugar

Directions

Drain the marrons and crumble them slightly. Pack a two-quart mold with a layer each of pistachio and chocolate ice cream, crumbled marrons, and peach ice cream, reserving the peach for the thick final layer. Cover the mold and freeze overnight.

To serve, prepare a meringue by beating the egg whites until they hold a peak and then gradually beating in the sugar. Continue to beat for 5 minutes.

Cover a bread board with heavy white paper. Cut a round of the sponge cake two inches larger than the bottom of the ice cream mold. Unmold the ice cream and center it on the cake round. Use a spatula to completely cover the ice cream and the cake with the meringue. Reserve some meringue and pipe it through a decorative nozzle of a pastry tube to form swirls and rosettes on top of the dessert. Dust with sugar and place in an oven preheated to 450 degrees F., until the meringue is delicately browned (about 5 minutes). Slide the Baked Alaska onto a serving plate and serve immediately.

almond
jello
surprise*

(Serves 8 to 10)

Rather exotic and quite refreshing is this delicate dessert.

APRICOTS
Ingredients

36 Dried apricots
1 Cup apricot nectar
½ Cup cold water
½ Cup granulated sugar
½ Teaspoon rose water

* Prepare apricots 2 days in advance of serving.

Directions

Wash the dried apricots. Mix the remaining ingredients. Add the apricots to the liquid and place in the refrigerator for 2 days. Stir occasionally.

ALMOND JELLO
Ingredients

1½ Cups milk
3 Tablespoons granulated sugar
2½ Cups water
1½ Tablespoons unflavored gelatin
4 Tablespoons cold water
3 Teaspoons almond extract

Directions

Mix the milk, the sugar, and the water in a saucepan. Heat, stirring to dissolve the sugar, but do *not* boil. Soften the gelatin in 4 tablespoons of cold water and stir it into the hot liquid until the gelatin has completely dissolved. Cool to room temperature and stir in the almond extract. Pour into a cake pan and chill until it has gelled.

TO ASSEMBLE THE DESSERT
Ingredients

2 20-Ounce cans litchi nuts
1½ Cups heavy cream
5 Tablespoons granulated sugar
¼ Teaspoon rose water

Directions

Drain the litchi nuts. Drain the apricots and cut each into quarters. Cut the jello into half-inch cubes. Chill these ingredients separately.

One-half hour prior to serving, whip the heavy cream until it thickens slightly. Sprinkle in the sugar and continue to beat until the cream is fairly stiff. Stir in the rose water.

Mix the litchi nuts and the apricots in a large glass bowl. Use a rubber spatula to fold in the jello cubes and the heavy cream. Serve very cold in small glass bowls.

pineapple
bombe

The first step toward trouble-free hostessing is to prepare this frosty Pineapple Bombe one day in advance of that next company dinner.

Ingredients

1½ Cups granulated sugar	¼ Cup chopped green candied cherries
1 Cup water	¾ Cup chopped marrons glacés
7 Egg yolks	1½ Cups finely diced fresh pineapple
2-Inch piece of vanilla bean	3 Tablespoons crème de cacao liqueur
3 Cups heavy cream	4 Rings of candied pineapple
1 Teaspoon vanilla extract	4 Whole green candied cherries

Directions

Bring the sugar and water to a boil, stirring constantly. Boil for 5 minutes and cool somewhat. In the top of a double boiler, beat the egg yolks with an electric beater until they are light in color. Continue beating as you gradually whip in the syrup. Split the vanilla bean, scrape out the fine seeds, and add them to the custard. Beat over hot, but not boiling, water until the mixture is thick and creamy. Strain. Cool over cracked ice, stirring occasionally. Meanwhile, whip the heavy cream until it is stiff, and fold in the vanilla extract. Fold the whipped cream into the cooled custard. Drain the marrons glacés, chop them coarsely, and fold them, with the chopped candied cherries, into one-half the vanilla mousse. Line the bottom of a chilled 2½-quart bombe mold with this mixture. Freeze for three hours. Meanwhile, finely chop the fresh pineapple and mix it with the crème de cacao. Fold this into the remaining mousse. Fill the rest of the bombe mold with this mixture. Cover with buttered wax paper and adjust the cover of the mold. Freeze overnight. When ready to serve, unmold the bombe and garnish it with half slices of candied pineapple and halved green candied cherries.

frozen peppermint mousse

(Serves 8 to 10)

Children and adults are equally enthusiastic about this refreshing frozen dessert. This crunchy peppermint mousse must be prepared one day in advance of serving. Can you think of a better way to lighten the work load on dinner-party day?

Ingredients

1½ Cups granulated sugar
1 Cup water
7 Egg yolks
2-Inch piece of vanilla bean
3 Cups heavy cream
1 Teaspoon vanilla extract
½ Pound red-and-white peppermint candies

Directions

Bring the sugar and water to a boil, stirring constantly. Boil for 5 minutes and cool somewhat. In the top of a double boiler, beat the egg yolks with an electric beater until they are light in color. Continue beating as you gradually whip in the syrup. Split the vanilla bean, scrape out the fine seeds, and add them to the custard. Beat over hot, but not boiling, water until the mixture is thick and creamy. Strain. Cool over cracked ice, stirring occasionally. Meanwhile, whip the heavy cream until it is stiff, and stir in the vanilla extract. Fold the whipped cream into the cooled custard. Crush the peppermint candies with a rolling pin and fold them into the mousse. Turn the mixture into a fancy mold, cover it with buttered wax paper, and freeze overnight. At serving time, decorate it gaily with peppermint candies.

crêpes with chocolate sauce

(Serves 8 to 10)

My favorite crêpe recipe is this one. Here the crêpes are filled with pistachio nuts, topped with orange-chocolate sauce, and served with ice cream and whipped cream; tremendously rich, but utterly delicious. Why not try it? It may become your *favorite too.*

CRÊPES

Ingredients

1 Cup all-purpose flour
1 Tablespoon granulated sugar
¼ Teaspoon salt
3 Eggs
3 Egg yolks
2 Cups milk
2 Tablespoons butter
1 Teaspoon brandy

Directions

Mix together the flour, the sugar, and the salt. Beat the eggs and the egg yolks, add the milk, and mix well. Gradually add the dry ingredients to the egg-milk mixture, beating constantly until smooth. Melt the butter and stir it, with the brandy, into the batter. For best results, allow the batter to stand for 2 hours before cooking the crêpes. Brush a 4-inch skillet (or crêpe pan) with melted butter and, when it is hot, pour in one tablespoon of batter. Tip and tilt the pan over the heat so that the batter will cover the entire bottom of the skillet. When the crêpe is lightly browned on the bottom, turn it and lightly brown the other side. Repeat the process, until all of the batter has been turned into thin golden crêpes. Stack the crêpes on a plate and cover them with waxed paper while you prepare the filling.

PISTACHIO NUT FILLING
Ingredients

1 Cup finely chopped pistachio nuts
5 Tablespoons churned (or whipped or blended) honey
2 Tablespoons plus 2 teaspoons Grand Marnier

Directions

Place the above ingredients in a bowl and mix well.

ORANGE-CHOCOLATE SAUCE
Ingredients

4 Squares bitter chocolate
2 Tablespoons butter
2 Tablespoons Grand Marnier
1 Cup granulated sugar
1 Cup heavy cream

Directions

Place the chocolate, the butter, and the Grand Marnier in a heavy skillet over a low flame until the chocolate is melted. Combine the sugar and the cream and add it to the melted chocolate. Stir over a low flame until the sauce reaches the boiling point. Reduce the heat and cook over a low flame until the sauce thickens slightly.

TO SERVE
Ingredients

2 Cups sweetened whipped cream
2 Pints vanilla ice cream
¼ Cup melted butter

Directions

Spread a teaspoon or two of filling down the center of each crêpe, roll it, and place it on a serving platter. At serving time, carry the platter of rolled crêpes to the table with a bowl each of sweetened whipped cream, vanilla ice cream scooped into balls, and hot Orange-Chocolate sauce. Over the direct flame of a chafing dish, heat the butter in a large, shallow, copper crêpe pan and cook the rolled, filled crêpes until they are hot and slightly browned on both sides. Arrange two crêpes each on small plates, spoon some of the chocolate sauce over the crêpes, and place a heaping tablespoonful of whipped cream on one side of them and a ball of ice cream on the other. Serve immediately.

cream crêpes flamed with cointreau

(Serves 8 to 10)

The fussiest guest will break into smiles when presented with this rather special dessert treat. Soft, mellow vanilla cream is tucked into tender crêpes and the crêpes are flamed with Cointreau. The guests sample same, and corners of mouths turn upward forthwith.

CRÊPES
  Ingredients

1 Cup all-purpose flour
1 Tablespoon granulated sugar
¼ Teaspoon salt
3 Eggs
3 Egg yolks
2 Cups milk
2 Tablespoons butter
1 Teaspoon Cointreau
Grated outside yellow rind from one lemon
Grated outside orange rind from one orange
3 Tablespoons melted butter

Directions

Mix together the flour, the sugar, and the salt. Beat the eggs and the egg yolks, add the milk, and mix well. Gradually add the dry ingredients to the egg-milk mixture, beating constantly until smooth. Melt 1 teaspoon butter and stir it, with the Cointreau, into the batter. Grate the zest, or colored outer skin, from the fruit. (Be sure not to include any of the bitter white inner skin.) Stir the lemon and orange zest into the batter and allow it to stand for 2 hours before cooking the crêpes. Brush a 4-inch skillet (or crêpe pan) with melted butter and, when it is hot, pour in 1½ tablespoons of batter. Tip and tilt the pan over the heat so the batter will cover the entire bottom of the skillet. When the crêpe is lightly browned on the bottom, turn it and lightly brown the other side. Repeat the process, until all the batter has been turned into thin golden crêpes. Carefully stack the crêpes and cover with waxed paper until serving time.

CREAM FILLING
Ingredients

2 Tablespoons butter
1½ Cups sifted confectioners' sugar
A pinch of salt
2 Tablespoons heavy cream
½ Teaspoon vanilla extract

Directions

Cream the butter, add the salt and half of the sugar, and cream the mixture until it is perfectly smooth. Add the rest of the sugar and the heavy cream alternately. Stir in the vanilla extract.

TO SERVE
Ingredients

3 Tablespoons butter
½ Cup Cointreau

Directions

Spread a teaspoon or two of filling down the center of each crêpe. Roll, and arrange in two rows in a large, shallow, copper crêpe pan. In a chafing dish, at the table, melt the butter, add the Cointreau, and heat slightly. Set aflame. Place the pan of crêpes over the heat. Pour the flaming Cointreau over the crêpes. Serve immediately.

cherry crêpes with flaming ice cream

(Serves 8 to 10)

Just the dessert to show your guests how much you care!

CRÊPES
Ingredients

1 Cup all-purpose flour
1 Tablespoon granulated sugar
¼ Teaspoon salt
3 Eggs
3 Egg yolks
2 Cups milk
2 Tablespoons butter
1 Teaspoon brandy

Directions

Mix together the flour, the sugar, and the salt. Beat the eggs and egg yolks, add the milk, and mix well. Gradually add the dry ingredients to the egg-milk mixture, beating constantly until smooth. Melt the butter and stir 2 tablespoons with the brandy, into the batter. Let the batter stand for 2 hours before cooking the crêpes. Brush a 4-inch skillet with melted butter and, when it begins to bubble, pour in a tablespoon of batter. Tip and tilt the pan over the heat so that the batter will cover the entire bottom of the skillet. When the crêpe is lightly browned on the bottom, turn it and lightly brown the other side. Repeat the process, stacking the crêpes on a plate to be used later, until all the batter has been turned into thin golden crêpes. Cover the crêpes with waxed paper and allow them to remain at room temperature while you prepare the filling.

CHERRY FILLING
Ingredients

3 Cups pitted, tart cherries, drained
¾ Cup cherry juice
½ Cup granulated sugar

Directions

Place all the ingredients in a saucepan and cook until the syrup is thick.

TO SERVE
Ingredients

2 Tablespoons butter
1 Quart vanilla ice cream, quite firmly frozen*
½ Cup Cherry Heering

Directions

Spread a teaspoon or two of cherry filling down the center of each crêpe, roll, and place in bubbling butter, in a large, shallow, copper crêpe pan. Cook over medium flame until the crêpes are brown on the bottom, turn, and brown the other side. Arrange two rows of crêpes, side by side, in the pan and top every two or three crêpes with a scoop of ice cream.* Quickly carry the dessert to the table. In a chafing dish, over a direct flame, warm the Cherry Heering, set it aflame, and pour it over the crêpes and ice cream. Serve immediately.

* I suggest scooping and freezing the ice cream balls a day in advance.

steamed date and nut pudding with hard sauce

(Serves 8 to 10)

You might keep this recipe for spicy steamed pudding tucked away in your mind to bring forward when you're in need of a different dessert for a traditional Thanksgiving or Christmas dinner. This warm, comforting aftermath provides many of the pleasing qualities of pumpkin pie, but does so with a bit more flair.

STEAMED DATE AND NUT PUDDING
Ingredients
¾ Cup hot water
¼ Cup dark rum
8 Ounces pitted dates
½ Cup shortening
½ Cup granulated sugar
½ Cup unsulphured molasses
2 Eggs
1 Teaspoon baking soda
2 Cups all-purpose flour
1 Teaspoon baking powder
½ Teaspoon salt
¼ Teaspoon powdered cloves
¼ Teaspoon ginger
½ Teaspoon cinnamon
½ Teaspoon nutmeg
¾ Cup chopped walnuts

Directions

Bring the water and the rum to a boil. Pour this liquid over the dates and let stand for half an hour. Cream the shortening and the sugar, and beat in the molasses and the eggs. Drain the dates and reserve the liquid. Dissolve the baking soda in the liquid from the dates and add this to the shortening-molasses mixture. Sift the flour with the baking powder, the salt, and the spices. Add the dry ingredients to the creamed mixture and blend thoroughly. Chop the dates coarsely and add them, with the chopped nuts, to the batter. Butter a two-quart steamed pudding mold, pour in the batter, cover with aluminum foil, and secure the lid tightly. Put a wire rack in a large kettle and pour in enough boiling water to reach three-quarters of the way up the sides of the mold. If the mold seems prone to tip, crush aluminum foil and wedge it between the mold and the kettle. Cover the kettle with aluminum foil and a tight lid. Steam for 1¾ hours, adding more boiling water as needed. Remove the mold from the kettle of water, but do not discard the boiling water until you remove the lid from the pudding mold and peek in to see if the pudding is firm. If it is firm, discard all but two inches of the water and replace the covered pudding to keep it warm until serving time. If the pudding is still "mushy," recover the pudding, replace it in the boiling water, cover the pot, and continue to steam until the pudding is firm on top.

HARD SAUCE
Ingredients

3 Cups confectioners' sugar
½ Cup butter
3 Egg yolks
¼ Teaspoon nutmeg
1 Tablespoon rum
8 Whole dates
8 Walnut halves

Directions

Cream the sugar and the softened butter. Beat in the egg yolks, the nutmeg, and the rum. Chill.

TO SERVE THE PUDDING

Unmold onto a serving dish while still hot. Decorate with whole dates and walnut halves and points of Hard Sauce piped through a decorative nozzle of a pastry tube. Serve the remaining Hard Sauce in a separate dish.

imperial
rice
pudding

For some reason, rice pudding is seldom considered a dinner party dessert. This version, however, is sumptuous enough for even a royal table. What makes this pudding so special? Perhaps it's the ladyfingers that form the bottom layer, or the mellow vanilla custard that is spooned over these. Possibly it's the rice in its own orangey syrup, the layer of apricot jam, or even the mounds of sweetened whipped cream, heaped on the top. You may discover for yourself why this dessert is outstanding by merely following the recipe.

VANILLA CUSTARD
Ingredients

4 Eggs
½ Cup granulated sugar
1 Cup milk
½ Cup heavy cream
2-Inch piece of vanilla bean or ¾ teaspoon vanilla extract

Directions

Beat the eggs in the top of a double boiler. Add the sugar and continue beating until thoroughly mixed. Scald the milk and the heavy cream with the split vanilla bean and pour gradually into the egg mixture, stirring constantly. If vanilla extract is used, it must be added after the custard has cooled. Place over simmering water and stir until the mixture thickens. Do not overcook or the custard will curdle. Place the pan in cold water for a few seconds. Chill the custard, stirring occasionally.

RICE AND ORANGE SYRUP
Ingredients

1 Cup rice
2¾ Cups hot water
¾ Teaspoon salt
¾ Cup granulated sugar
2 Tablespoons butter
1 Lemon
1 Orange
4 Tablespoons rum

Directions

Wash the rice, using three changes of water. Place the washed rice, the hot water, and the salt in a saucepan. Cover and cook until the rice is soft, but not mushy. Meanwhile, mix the sugar and the butter in a small skillet. Squeeze the lemon and the orange, and strain the juice. Heat the sugar and the butter slowly, stirring constantly until the mixture is lightly browned. Add the juices and the rum and cook, stirring until the mixture becomes a well-blended syrup. Drain the rice thoroughly and fold it into the fruit syrup. Cool.

TO ASSEMBLE THE DESSERT
Ingredients

1½ Cups heavy cream
4 Tablespoons granulated sugar
½ Teaspoon almond extract
24 Ladyfingers
¾ Cup apricot jam or preserves

Directions

Beat the cream until it thickens slightly. Add the sugar, a little at a time, beating constantly. Continue to whip until the cream is thick. Fold in the almond extract. Line a glass dish with the ladyfingers and cover them with one-half of the chilled vanilla custard. Carefully spoon the rice-and-syrup mixture over the custard. Spread the rice with the apricot jam, pour the remaining vanilla custard over this, and top with whipped cream. Decorate with whipped cream rosettes piped around bits of apricot jam.

bread
pudding
with
meringue

(Serves 8)

This bread pudding has a special flavor secret—it is spiked generously with Grand Marnier! It also sports a party chapeau of frothy meringue. Here is the most humble of desserts, à la Cinderella, dressed for the ball.

P.S. The pudding is also delicious without the meringue.

PUDDING
Ingredients

6 Eggs
1 Cup granulated sugar
3 Cups milk
¼ Cup Grand Marnier
1 Teaspoon cinnamon
½ Teaspoon nutmeg
1 Teaspoon vanilla extract
16 Slices bread
4 Tablespoons butter

Directions

Beat together the eggs, the sugar, the milk, the Grand Marnier, the spices, and the vanilla extract. Slice the crusts from the bread, and lightly butter one side of each slice. Cut each slice of bread into three equal strips. Butter a soufflé dish and line the bottom and sides with buttered bread "fingers." Continue to lay in the bread "fingers" (one row going one way, and one going the other way) until the bowl is full. Break small pieces of bread to fill in any spaces. Beat the egg mixture again briefly, and pour it over the bread in the bowl. Bake the bread pudding for one hour in an oven preheated to 350 degrees F. Cool to room temperature.

MERINGUE
Ingredients

5 Egg whites
¼ Teaspoon cream of tartar
10 Tablespoons granulated sugar

Directions

Beat the egg whites until they are light and frothy. Add the cream of tartar. Beat again until the egg whites are stiff and hold a peak. Add the sugar, a little at a time, beating well after each addition. Continue to beat until the meringue is stiff and glossy. Heap the meringue on the cooled bread pudding. Spread it until it touches the sides of the dish. Use a spoon to swirl the meringue into high peaks. Bake in an oven preheated to 425 degrees F. for 5 to 6 minutes or until the top is attractively browned. Cool to room temperature. Serve at this temperature or chill.

macaroon
pudding

(Serves 8)

This old world pudding combines orange juice and cherry liqueur for an unpretentious but delicious dessert.

Ingredients

¾ Cup macaroon crumbs
1 Tablespoon unflavored gelatin
½ Cup water
4 Eggs
1 Cup granulated sugar
1 Cup milk

¼ Cup cherry liqueur
½ Cup orange juice
1 Tablespoon lemon juice
15 Whole blanched almonds
Bits of candied orange peel

Directions

Place the macaroon crumbs in the bottom of a soufflé dish. Soften the gelatin in cold water. Separate the egg whites from the yolks. In the top of a double boiler beat the egg yolks with the sugar until they are fluffy and smooth. Mix ¼ cup of cold milk with the sugar and the egg yolks. Scald the remaining ¾ cup of milk, add to the egg yolk mixture, and stir until the sugar is nearly dissolved and the liquid is smooth. Heat over boiling water, stirring constantly for about 10 minutes, or until the mixture is about twice the thickness of heavy cream. Mix the gelatin, the water, the liqueur, the orange juice, and the lemon juice. Stir this into the pudding in the double boiler. The mixture will be thin. Spoon 6 tablespoons of this liquid over the crumbs in the dish. Cool both the pudding and the crumbs. When the pudding is cool, *not cold,* beat the egg whites until they are stiff. Fold them into the pudding and pour into the soufflé dish. Chill for 10 hours. Decorate with a few macaroon crumbs and flowers formed of the whole almonds and bits of candied orange peel. Serve very cold.

apple pancake

Here is a dessert that is not only delightful to serve at an informal dinner, but also for lunch, for Sunday brunch, or as a spur-of-the-moment treat for your late-hour guests.

Ingredients

1 Cup all-purpose flour	2 Cups light cream
12 Tablespoons granulated sugar	4 Apples, peeled and thinly sliced
12 Tablespoons butter	6 Teaspoons lime juice
4 Eggs	1 Teaspoon cinnamon

Directions

Mix together the flour and 8 tablespoons of the sugar. Melt 6 tablespoons of the butter. Beat the eggs, the cream, and the 6 tablespoons of melted butter. Add the liquid mixture to the dry ingredients. Mix well. Let this stand for one hour. Peel, core, and slice the apples into quarter-inch-thick slices. Sprinkle the apple slices with 2 teaspoons of lime juice and gently toss. Melt one tablespoon of butter in a 10-inch skillet. Pour in ¼ of the pancake batter. Cook until golden brown, over medium flame. Do not turn. Slide the pancake onto a cookie sheet, uncooked side up, and repeat the process until all the batter has been used and you have four large pancakes cooked on one side, two pancakes each resting on a cookie sheet, uncooked side up. Now, when serving time arrives, arrange the apple slices on the uncooked tops of the pancakes. Sprinkle each apple-covered pancake with one tablespoon of sugar and ¼ teaspoon of cinnamon. Dot each with ½ tablespoon of butter and broil for 2 minutes. Remove the cookie sheets from the broiler and use a pancake turner to fold the pancakes in half, making sure not to tear them. Slide the pancakes onto a platter, sprinkle with a few grains of sugar and the remaining lime juice. At the table, cut the pancakes in half and serve warm.

chocolate bread pudding

(Serves 8)

Custardy chocolate—an interesting variation for bread pudding fanciers.

Ingredients

6 Eggs
1 Cup granulated sugar
2 Cups milk
1 Cup light cream
¼ Cup crème de cacao
½ Teaspoon cinnamon
½ Teaspoon nutmeg
1 Teaspoon vanilla extract
4 Ounces sweet chocolate
16 Slices white bread
4 Tablespoons butter
1 Cup semi-sweet chocolate bits

Directions

Beat together the eggs, the sugar, the milk, the light cream, the crème de cacao, the spices, and the vanilla extract. Melt the 4 ounces of sweet chocolate in the top of a double boiler over boiling water. Stir the melted chocolate into the egg mixture. Slice the crusts from the bread, and lightly butter one side of each slice. Cut each slice of bread into three equal strips. Butter a soufflé dish and line the bottom and sides with buttered bread "fingers." Scatter a few chocolate bits over the bread strips. Continue to lay in the bread "fingers" (one row going one way, and one going the other way) and chocolate bits until the bowl is full. Break small pieces of bread to fill in any spaces. Beat the egg-chocolate mixture again *briefly*. (Do not allow the mixture to become too frothy or it will not saturate the bread properly.) Pour the liquid over the bread in the bowl and bake the pudding for 1 hour in an oven preheated to 350 degrees F. Serve warm (*not* hot).

little somethings

ladyfingers

(Makes about 3 dozen—serves 8 to 10)

For a treat as light and delicate as the name implies, try these low-calorie "fingers."

Ingredients

6 Egg yolks
¼ Cup granulated sugar
4 Egg whites
½ Cup granulated sugar
1 Cup all-purpose flour
¼ Cup confectioners' sugar

Directions

Beat the egg yolks until they are light in color. Stir in ¼ cup granulated sugar and beat until creamy. In another bowl beat the egg whites until they are foamy. Add ½ cup of granulated sugar, and beat again until this meringue stands in stiff peaks. Fold this into the egg mixture. Sift the flour over the batter and gently fold it in. Line baking sheets with white paper. Use a pastry tube without a nozzle to pipe "fingers" of batter onto the paper. Sprinkle with very fine granulated sugar, or confectioners' sugar shaken from a very fine sieve. Bake for 10 minutes in an oven preheated to 350 degrees F. Loosen the ladyfingers from the paper at once, and let them dry for 12 hours.

little somethings

beignets soufflés

(Serves 8 to 10)

Here is positive proof that good things can come in small packages. These flavorful puffs are light and lovely, and easy to make.

PÂTE À CHOUX
Ingredients

1 Cup water
½ Cup butter
1¼ Cups all-purpose flour
½ Teaspoon orange extract
1 Tablespoon rum
5 Eggs
Hot fat for deep frying
¾ Cup confectioners' sugar

Directions

Boil the water and the butter together in a saucepan. Add the flour all at one time and stir rapidly with a wooden spoon until the dough leaves the sides of the pan and forms a ball. Remove the pan from the heat and stir in the orange extract and the rum. Beat in the eggs one at a time, beating thoroughly after each addition. Continue to beat the mixture until it is smooth and has a sheen. Use two tablespoons to form the Pâte à Choux into balls. As the balls are formed, drop them, a few at a time, into deep, hot fat (370 degrees F.). Fry until lightly browned. They will turn of their own accord if there is enough room in the fryer. Drain well and sprinkle with confectioners' sugar. Serve hot.

desserts
to serve
ten to twelve
persons

A party that involves ten to twelve persons tends to be somewhat more of an "occasion" than the more intimate gathering of six or eight guests. The recipes that follow are a bit more spectacular for precisely that reason.

pineapple-cream cheese torte

(Serves 10 to 12)

An unusual torte is this one with crunchy rolled-oat layers nestled under Cream Cheese Cake and Pineapple-Raisin Filling.

PINEAPPLE-RAISIN FILLING

Ingredients

2 Cups golden raisins, loosely packed
½ Cup granulated sugar
1 Cup canned crushed pineapple (with juice)
3 Tablespoons cornstarch
½ Cup cold water

Directions

Chop the raisins until each one has been cut into quarters or smaller. Mix the chopped raisins, the sugar, the crushed pineapple, and the pineapple juice in a medium-size saucepan. Stir the corn-starch into the water and add it to the fruit in the saucepan. Cook over medium heat, stirring constantly, until the filling is very thick (about 15 minutes). Cool.

CREAM CHEESE CAKE FILLING
Ingredients
16 Ounces cream cheese
1 Pinch salt
½ Split vanilla bean or 1 teaspoon vanilla extract
2 Eggs
2 Egg yolks
½ Cup granulated sugar

Directions
Beat the cream cheese in a small bowl until it is light and fluffy. Add the salt. Scrape the tiny seeds from the split vanilla bean and stir these into the cheese. Beat the eggs, the egg yolks, and the sugar together for several minutes or until smooth and light yellow in color. Beat these into the cheese mixture, pausing several times to scrape the bottom of the bowl.

ROLLED-OAT LAYERS
Ingredients
10 Tablespoons butter
½ Teaspoon cinnamon
1¾ Cups old-fashioned rolled oats
1½ Tablespoons all-purpose flour
1½ Teaspoons baking powder
1 Egg
1 Egg yolk
1 Cup granulated sugar

Directions
Melt the butter and place it in a large bowl with the cinnamon and the rolled oats. Stir. Sprinkle the flour and the baking powder over this. Mix well. In a small bowl, beat the egg, the egg yolk, and the sugar until they are fluffy, and beat this mixture into the dry ingredients. Butter and flour the bottoms of three spring-form pans (or the backs of three 9-inch cake pans). Spread the batter to within a half inch of the edges of the pans. Bake for 10

minutes in an oven preheated to 350 degrees F. Cool the layers on the pans.

TO ASSEMBLE THE CAKE

If you are using spring-form pans, spoon ⅓ of the cream cheese filling over each of the rolled-oat layers and bake in an oven preheated to 350 degrees F. for 30 minutes or until the center is firm to the touch.

If you have baked the layers on the backs of the cake pans, cover them thinly with the cream cheese mixture and then spoon two additional tablespoonfuls onto the centers of each layer. Bake for 15 minutes in an oven preheated to 350 degrees F.

Remove one layer from the oven and, while it is still hot, use a sharp knife and a spatula to loosen it gently and slide it onto the serving plate. Carefully spoon and spread half of the Pineapple-Raisin Filling over this, being careful not to damage the cream cheese filling.

Take another cheese-covered layer from the oven. Gently remove it from the pan as described above and slide it onto the fruit filling of the bottom layer. Spread this with the remaining fruit filling.

Remove the third layer from the oven and, before placing it on the torte, top it with the following Streusel Topping.

STREUSEL TOPPING
  Ingredients

6 Tablespoons all-purpose flour
6 Tablespoons light brown sugar
¼ Cup butter

  Directions

Mix the flour and the sugar in a small mixing bowl. Cut in the butter with a pastry cutter or two knives until the mixture is reduced to coarse crumbs. Sprinkle these crumbs over the remaining cheese-covered layer and broil (at about five inches from the flame) until the crumbs are lightly browned. (Be sure to watch over this process carefully. This Streusel Topping burns easily.) Remove the layer from the broiler and, while it is hot, gently loosen it and slide it onto the top of the cake. This may be refrigerated, but it is best when served at room temperature.

96

strawberry trifle

The trifle is a dessert which the English hold dear, and for a very good reason. This mellow blending of strawberries, ladyfingers, and vanilla custard couldn't be more delicious.

Ingredients

4 Egg yolks
½ Cup granulated sugar
1 Cup heavy cream
1 Cup milk
2-Inch piece of vanilla bean
3 Dozen ladyfingers
¼ Cup apricot jam

¼ Cup sherry or madeira
1 Quart ripe fresh strawberries
½ Cup heavy cream
1 Tablespoon plus 2 teaspoons granulated sugar
¼ Teaspoon vanilla

Directions

Beat the egg yolks until they are light in color. Stir in ½ cup of sugar. Scald a cup of heavy cream and a cup of milk with the split vanilla bean. Add the scalded liquid, a little at a time, to the egg-yolk mixture. Cook this mixture in the top of a double boiler over hot water, stirring constantly, until it coats the spoon. Do not overcook, or the custard will curdle. Strain the custard and cool it, stirring occasionally.

Line the bottom and sides of a glass serving bowl with ladyfingers. Sprinkle with sherry or Madeira. Heat the apricot jam. Use a pastry brush to lightly cover the ladyfingers with the jam. Spoon half of the cooled custard over these sponge fingers. Place over this another row of ladyfingers, top these with thin strawberry slices, and cover with the remaining custard.

Whip the remaining ½ cup of heavy cream until it is fairly thick. Gradually add the remaining sugar and the vanilla. Spread the sweetened whipped cream over the custard. Top with sliced berries and chill. Serve cold.

summer
trifle

(Serves 10 to 12)

This cool, ladylike dessert is fashioned from raspberries, ice cream, vanilla custard, and light-as-a-feather sponge layers.

SPONGE CAKE
Ingredients

8 Egg yolks
¾ Cup granulated sugar
6 Tablespoons ground almonds
6 Tablespoons all-purpose flour
5 Egg whites
1 Lemon
5 Drops almond extract

Directions

Cream the egg yolks and the sugar until they are light and fluffy. Stir in the ground almonds and the flour. Beat the egg whites until they hold a stiff peak. Fold the beaten egg whites into the egg yolk-nut mixture. Squeeze and strain the juice of the lemon. Add the almond extract and the lemon juice to the batter and mix gently, but well. Divide the batter evenly between three buttered 9-inch cake pans and bake in an oven preheated to 375 degrees

F. for 20 to 25 minutes or until the center of the cake springs back when lightly pressed with the finger. Cool.

VANILLA CUSTARD
Ingredients

5 Egg yolks
½ Cup granulated sugar
1 Cup milk
1 Cup light cream
½ Vanilla bean

Directions

Beat the egg yolks and the sugar in the top of a double boiler until the mixture is light and creamy. In another saucepan, scald the milk and the cream with the split vanilla bean. Pour this into the egg yolk mixture, a little at a time, stirring constantly. Cook over hot water, stirring continually until the custard coats a spoon. Do not allow to boil. Strain the custard and cool, stirring occasionally.

TO ASSEMBLE THE DESSERT
Ingredients

1 Quart raspberries
1 Cup granulated sugar
1 Quart rich vanilla ice cream
¼ Cup rum
½ Cup sherry
1 Cup heavy cream
3 Tablespoons granulated sugar

Directions

Wash the raspberries and reserve ½ cup of berries for garnish. Crush the remaining berries with 1 cup of sugar. Soften the ice cream slightly and stir in the rum.

Line a deep 10-inch crystal bowl with alternate layers of the crushed raspberries, 9-inch circles of sponge cake sprinkled with sherry, semi-soft ice cream, and vanilla custard, in that order. Work quickly so the ice cream doesn't melt. Freeze for an hour. Whip the cream with the 3 tablespoons sugar. Ten minutes before serving time, remove the Summer Trifle from the freezer, garnish with swirls and rosettes of whipped cream. Decorate with the reserved whole raspberries. Serve immediately.

rum
cake

I believe this to be the most delicate, the most delicious, rum cake that one can possibly make.

SPONGE CAKE
Ingredients

8 Egg yolks
¾ Cup granulated sugar
6 Tablespoons ground almonds
6 Tablespoons all-purpose flour
5 Egg whites
5 Drops almond extract
1 Lemon

Directions

Cream the egg yolks and the sugar until light and fluffy. Stir in the ground almonds and the flour. Beat the egg whites until they hold a stiff peak. Fold the beaten egg whites into the egg yolk-nut mixture. Squeeze and strain the juice of the lemon. Add the almond extract and the lemon juice to the batter and mix gently, but well. Divide the batter evenly among three buttered 9-inch cake pans and bake for 20 to 25 minutes in an oven preheated to 350 degrees F. until the center of the cake springs back when lightly pressed with the finger. Cool.

FILLING
Ingredients

4 Eggs
½ Cup granulated sugar
1 Cup milk
½ Cup heavy cream
½ Teaspoon vanilla extract

Directions

Beat the eggs in the top of a double boiler. Add the sugar and continue beating until thoroughly mixed. Scald the milk and heavy cream and pour gradually into the eggs, stirring constantly. Place over simmering water and stir until the mixture thickens slightly. Do not overcook or the custard will curdle. Place the pan in cold water for a few seconds and then stir in the vanilla extract. Chill the custard, stirring occasionally.

TO ASSEMBLE THE CAKE
Ingredients

½ Cup rum
½ Cup apricot preserves
⅓ Cup seedless raspberry jelly
1 Cup heavy cream
3 Tablespoons granulated sugar
½ Teaspoon vanilla
12 Candied cherries (red and green)
2 Tablespoons grated semi-sweet chocolate

Directions

Place one layer of sponge cake on a large plate. Sprinkle it with half the rum. Spread the layer with the apricot preserves and spoon over it half of the chilled vanilla custard. Place the second layer of cake on the custard and spread it with raspberry jelly and the remainder of the custard. Add the third layer of cake and sprinkle it with the remainder of the rum.

Whip the heavy cream until it begins to thicken. Add the sugar, a little at a time, and continue to beat until the cream is fairly stiff. Add the vanilla extract and beat for a few seconds more. Use a pastry tube to pipe swirls and rosettes around the top of the cake. Decorate with halved candied cherries and grated semi-sweet chocolate.

apricot-cream cake

Here is a delicate dessert, the base of which is home-baked ladyfingers. There are two fillings: one smooth, thick, vanilla cream, one tart apricot. Both are perfect escorts for such ladylike company. This is a cake that's well worth remembering.

LADYFINGERS*

Ingredients

6 Egg yolks
¼ Cup granulated sugar
4 Egg whites

½ Cup granulated sugar
1 Cup all-purpose flour
¼ Cup confectioners' sugar

Directions

Beat the egg yolks until they are light in color. Stir in ¼ cup of granulated sugar and beat until creamy. In another bowl, beat the egg whites until they are foamy. Add ½ cup of granulated sugar to them and beat again until this meringue stands in stiff peaks. Fold this into the egg yolk mixture. Sift the flour over the batter and gently fold it in. Line baking sheets with white paper. Use a pastry tube without a nozzle to pipe "fingers" of batter onto the paper. Sprinkle with fine granulated sugar or confectioners' sugar shaken from a very fine sieve. Bake for 10 minutes in an oven preheated to 350 degrees F. Loosen the ladyfingers from the paper at once and let them dry for 12 hours.

VANILLA CREAM

Ingredients

⅓ Cup granulated sugar
4 Tablespoons cornstarch
6 Egg yolks

2 Cups milk
2-Inch piece of vanilla bean
(or 1 teaspoon vanilla extract)

Directions

Place the sugar, the cornstarch, and the egg yolks in the top of a double boiler. Mix well. Use another saucepan to scald the milk.

* You may use "grocery store" ladyfingers, but home baked are better.

Pour the scalded milk, with the vanilla bean, slowly into the egg yolk mixture, stirring rapidly and constantly. (If vanilla extract is used, it must be added after the vanilla custard is chilled.) Cook the mixture over boiling water, stirring constantly, until the cream is very thick. Remove the vanilla bean and strain the cream into an oven-proof bowl. Chill, stirring occasionally to prevent a skin from forming on top of the cream.

APRICOT FILLING
Ingredients

1 Cup dried apricots, tightly packed   1 Tablespoon unflavored gelatin
1 Cup water   ¼ Cup water
1¼ Cups granulated sugar

Directions

Place the washed apricots and a cup of water in a medium-sized saucepan. Boil gently for 10 minutes. Add the sugar and continue to boil, stirring constantly until the apricot mixture is *very* thick. Soften the gelatin in ¼ cup of water. Add it to the hot apricot mixture and stir until it is dissolved. Chill.

TO ASSEMBLE THE CAKE
Ingredients

4 Tablespoons Cointreau   2 Cups heavy cream
9 Tablespoons water   ⅓ Cup granulated sugar
4 Tablespoons granulated sugar   1 Teaspoon Cointreau

Directions

Mix 4 tablespoons of Cointreau, 9 tablespoons of water, and 4 tablespoons of granulated sugar in a narrow glass. Dip enough ladyfingers in this liquid to line the bottom of an 11-inch springform pan. Break the ladyfingers and fit them in where it is necessary to fill up the spaces. Spread half of the chilled Vanilla Cream over the bottom layer of ladyfingers. Top this with half of the Apricot Filling. Repeat the process, dipping the ladyfingers, fitting them, and spreading them with Vanilla Cream and Apricot Filling.

Beat the heavy cream until it has thickened slightly. Gradually beat in ⅓ cup of sugar and continue beating until the cream is quite stiff. Stir in the teaspoon of Cointreau. Ice the cake with the whipped cream and use a pastry tube with a fluted nozzle to decorate the top. Chill for at least 3 hours before serving.

angel
food cake
with
lime
cream

(Serves 10 to 12)

Split an angel food cake into three layers, spread those pristine layers with tart Lime Cream, frost with sweetened whipped cream, decorate with candied peel, and serve with confidence.

ANGEL FOOD CAKE

Ingredients

1½ Cups egg whites
¼ Teaspoon cream of tartar
1½ Cups granulated sugar
½ Teaspoon almond extract
1 Teaspoon vanilla extract
1 Cup cake flour

Directions

Beat the egg whites until they are foamy. Sprinkle the cream of tartar over these and beat again until the whites are stiff, glossy, and stand in peaks. Fold in the sugar, ¼ cup at a time and, after this, fold in the almond and vanilla extracts. Sift the cake flour three or four times. Sift ¼ cup of this sifted flour over the egg white mixture and fold in quickly. Continue this sifting and folding until the flour has all been used. Do not overmix. Gently spread the batter in an ungreased 10-inch tube pan. Bake for 35 to 40 minutes in an oven preheated to 375 degrees F. Test the cake by pressing the top gently with your finger. When the cake springs back from this pressure, it is done. Cool the cake in the pan. Meanwhile, prepare the Lime Cream.

LIME CREAM
Ingredients

¾ Cup unstrained lime juice
2¼ Cups granulated sugar
1 Cup cold water
3 Tablespoons cornstarch

4 Egg yolks
1 Tablespoon butter
1 Drop green food coloring

Mix the lime juice, the sugar, the water, and the cornstarch in the top of a double boiler. Cook over a medium flame, stirring constantly, until the mixture is thick and clear. Beat the egg yolks in a Pyrex bowl. Pour the hot lime mixture over them, stirring constantly. Add the butter and the food coloring and mix well. Return the Lime Cream to the top of the double boiler and cook for 5 minutes over lightly bubbling water, stirring constantly. Do not allow to come to a boil. Chill thoroughly.

TO ASSEMBLE THE CAKE
Ingredients

1½ Cups heavy cream
3 Tablespoons granulated sugar
Candied lime peel

Directions

Whip the cream until it begins to thicken. Continue beating as you sprinkle in the sugar. Whip until fairly stiff. Spread the chilled Lime Cream between the layers of the cake. Ice the top and sides of the assembled cake with swirls of whipped cream and decorate the top with strips of candied lime peel, arranged in an overlapping pattern.

Refrigerate for 2 to 3 hours. Serve very cold.

chocolate parson

(Serves 10 to 12)

This variation of "Tipsy Parson" combines angel food cake, chocolate custard, whipped cream, and toasted almond slivers.

CAKE

Ingredients

1½ Cups egg whites
¼ Teaspoon cream of tartar
1½ Cups granulated sugar

½ Teaspoon almond extract
1 Teaspoon vanilla extract
1 Cup cake flour

Directions

Beat the egg whites until they are foamy. Sprinkle the cream of tartar over these and beat again until the whites are stiff and glossy and stand in peaks. Fold in the sugar, ¼ cup at a time and, after completing this, fold in the almond and vanilla extracts. Sift the cake flour 3 or 4 times. Sift ¼ cup of this flour over the egg white mixture and fold it in quickly. Continue this sifting and folding until the flour has all been used. Do not overmix. Gently spread the batter in an ungreased 10-inch tube pan. Bake for 35 to 40 minutes in an oven preheated to 375 degrees F. Test by pressing the top of the cake gently with your finger. When the cake springs back from this pressure, it is done. Cool the cake in the pan, inverting it over a wire rack. Be sure to prop up the pan so that the cake itself does not touch the rack. When it is completely cool, carefully loosen the cake with the spatula, and turn the cake out of the pan onto a large shallow glass bowl.

CHOCOLATE CUSTARD FILLING

Ingredients

1½ Cups milk
1-Inch piece of vanilla bean
3 Egg yolks

⅓ Cup granulated sugar
1 Teaspoon all-purpose flour
2 Squares semi-sweet chocolate

Directions

Scald the milk with the vanilla bean. Beat the egg yolks until they are a light lemon color. Beat in the sugar and continue beating until the mixture is smooth. Mix in the flour. Melt the chocolate in the top of a double boiler over boiling water. Allow the melted chocolate to cool slightly while you finish preparing the custard. Pour the scalded milk slowly into the egg mixture, stirring constantly. Pour this into the melted chocolate, stir until no streaks of pure chocolate can be seen, and cook the mixture over simmering water until it thickens enough to coat the back of a spoon. Strain the custard and remove the piece of vanilla bean. Cool the custard and then chill it.

WHIPPED CREAM ICING

Ingredients

1 Cup heavy cream   ¼ Teaspoon almond extract
2 Tablespoons granulated sugar

Directions

Whip the cream until it holds a soft peak. Gradually add the sugar while continuing to whip the cream. When the cream is quite stiff, gently stir in the almond extract. Place this in the refrigerator until needed.

TRIMMINGS

Ingredients

2 Squares semi-sweet chocolate   1¼ Cups toasted almonds,
1 Tablespoon heavy cream   coarsely chopped
                                      Sherry

Directions

Melt the chocolate over hot water. Mix in the heavy cream. Cool slightly.

TO ASSEMBLE THE DESSERT

Slice the angel food cake into three horizontal slices. (This means you will have three very large angel food "doughnuts.") Place the bottom layer of the cake on the shallow serving bowl. Sprinkle with the sherry and the almonds. (Do not use too many almonds, since they will be used on the outside of the cake also.) Spread a layer of custard over this and cover it with the middle slice of the cake. Repeat the process by sprinkling this layer with the sherry and the almonds, and spreading with the Chocolate Custard Filling. Cover this with the top angel food layer and sprinkle the top and the sides of the assembled cake with sherry. Generously ice the entire cake with the whipped cream. Drip the melted chocolate over the top and the sides of the cake. Gently press the remaining chopped almonds on the top and sides of the cake. Pour the remaining Chocolate Custard Filling around the cake. Serve very cold.

orange angel cake with chocolate bits

(Serves 10 to 12)

The recipe for this birthday party cake evolved over a period of years. It combines two foods children love dearly—angel food cake and chocolate bits. It is most enjoyable between birthdays, too.

CAKE
Ingredients

1½ Cups egg whites
¼ Teaspoon cream of tartar
1½ Cups granulated sugar
1 Teaspoon orange extract
½ Teaspoon vanilla extract
1 Cup cake flour
½ Cup semi-sweet chocolate bits
¼ Cup chopped candied orange peel

Directions

Beat the egg whites until they are foamy. Sprinkle the cream of tartar over these and beat again until they are stiff, glossy, and stand in peaks. Fold in the sugar, ¼ cup at a time, and, after completing this, fold in the orange and vanilla extracts. Sift the cake flour three or four times. Sift ¼ cup of this flour over the egg white mixture, and fold it in quickly. Continue this sifting and folding until all of the flour has been used. Do not overmix. Fold in the chocolate bits and the candied orange peel. Gently spread the batter in an ungreased 10-inch tube pan. Bake for 35 to 40 minutes in an oven preheated to 375 degrees F. Test by pressing the top of the cake gently with your finger. When the cake springs back from this pressure, it is done. Cool in the pan.

ORANGE GLAZE*
Ingredients

1 Cup confectioners' sugar
3 Tablespoons orange juice
1 Egg white
60 Semi-sweet chocolate bits

Directions

Mix the sugar and the orange juice until smooth. Beat the egg white until it is frothy and add it to the sugar mixture. Beat at high speed for several minutes. Ice the top of the cooled cake, allowing icing to drip over the edges and run down the sides of the cake. Arrange the chocolate bits around the top edges of the cake.

* If your children are chocolate fanciers, ice the cake with rich chocolate frosting.

devil's food cake

(Serves 10 to 12)

This dark, rich, three-layer devil's food cake is enhanced by a thin layer of almond paste tucked neatly under its glossy fudge icing.

CAKE
Ingredients

½ Cup butter
2 Cups brown sugar (firmly packed)
½ Cup dark corn syrup
3 Eggs
3 Squares unsweetened chocolate
2¼ Cups cake flour,
    measured after sifting
2 Teaspoons baking soda

½ Teaspoon salt
½ Cup milk
1½ Teaspoons butter
1½ Teaspoons lemon juice
1 Cup boiling water
1½ Teaspoons vanilla extract
1 Teaspoon almond extract

Directions

Cream the butter until it is fluffy and light in color. Gradually cream in the brown sugar until the mixture is smooth. Beat in the corn syrup. Add the eggs, one at a time, beating well after each addition. Melt the chocolate over hot water and stir it into the brown sugar-egg mixture. Sift the flour, measure it, and sift it again with the baking soda and salt. Add the 1½ teaspoons of butter to the milk and stir over *low* heat until the butter has melted. Cool. Add the lemon juice to the milk and stir. Stir portions of the dry ingredients into the brown sugar mixture alternately with the soured milk, ending with the flour. Add the cup of boiling water and the vanilla and almond extracts. Grease and lightly flour three 8-inch cake pans. Divide the batter between the three pans and bake the cakes in an oven preheated to 375 degrees F. for 25 to 30 minutes. Cool the layers for 5 minutes, remove them from the pans, and place them on racks to cool.

ALMOND PASTE
Ingredients

1¼ Cups confectioners' sugar, measured after sifting
1 Cup ground almonds
1 Egg white
½ Teaspoon almond extract

Directions

Measure all ingredients and place them in a mixing bowl. Use your fingers to blend the mixture until it is the consistency of dough. If it is too crumbly to form a ball, add a bit more egg white. If it is too sticky, mix in a tablespoon of the confectioners' sugar and let the paste dry slightly. Reserve a small amount for trim, and roll the rest of the Almond Paste between two sheets of wax paper until it is the same size as the top of the cake.

FUDGE ICING
Ingredients

1¼ Cups granulated sugar
4 Ounces unsweetened chocolate
2 Ounces sweet chocolate
12 Tablespoons milk
3 Tablespoons butter
1 Teaspoon almond extract

Directions

In a saucepan, combine all ingredients except the almond extract. Cook the mixture over medium heat, stirring constantly until it forms a soft mass that can be rolled between the fingers when a bit is dropped into a cup of cold water. Remove from the flame and beat in the almond extract. Cool completely.

TO ASSEMBLE THE CAKE

Frost two of the layers with the cooled Fudge Icing. Stack the layers. Peel off the top sheet of paper from the Almond Paste and invert it on top of the cake. Peel off the other sheet of paper. Spread the remaining frosting over the top and the sides of the cake. Decorate with whole, blanched almonds set like flowers on the top of the cake. Roll out the reserved piece of Almond Paste and cut it into thin strips. Connect the almond flowers with curved strips of almond paste.

seven-layer
cake

Seven layers of cake with chocolate cream, marmalade, and toasted nuts make this seven times more delicious than the average dessert.

CAKE
Ingredients

7 Eggs
¾ Cup plus 2 tablespoons granulated sugar
1 Cup plus 1 tablespoon all-purpose flour

Directions

Beat the egg whites stiff with ¼ cup plus 2 tablespoons sugar. Beat the egg yolks with the remaining ½ cup of sugar until they are pale lemon in color and creamy in texture. Fold the beaten egg whites into the egg yolk mixture. Sift a light dusting of flour over this batter, fold the flour in, and repeat the process until all of it has been used. Butter and flour the *backs* of several 9-inch cake pans and spread them *thinly* with the batter. Bake in an oven pre-heated to 350 degrees F. for 15 minutes. Carefully slip a sharp knife under the layers to remove them from the tins, and let them cool in a dry place. Wash and dry the cake pans, and repeat the process until you have seven cool layers. If any of the layers is too high in the center or too thick in any one place, trim it with a large, sharp knife.

CHOCOLATE CREAM FILLING
Ingredients

½ Cup granulated sugar
2 Eggs plus one egg yolk
2 Ounces semi-sweet chocolate

2 Tablespoons Grand Marnier
¾ Cup butter

Directions

Beat the sugar, the eggs, the egg yolk, and the grated chocolate in the top of a double boiler over simmering water until it is creamy and smooth, and the chocolate is melted. Chill the mixture and stir in the Grand Marnier. Cream the butter and beat it into the chocolate. Cool.

CARAMEL GLAZE
Ingredients

½ Cup granulated sugar   ½ Cup water

Directions

Boil the sugar and water in a heavy skillet until it turns golden brown. Select the best layer and quickly spread it with the caramel glaze. As the glaze is hardening, score it with a knife to mark it into serving portions.

TO ASSEMBLE THE CAKE
Ingredients

1¾ Cups Brazil nuts
2½ Tablespoons butter

¼ Cup orange marmalade

Directions

Cut the Brazil nuts into thin slices. Melt the butter in a baking pan, stir in the nuts, and bake them in an oven preheated to 350°F. until they are golden brown.

Place one layer of the cake on the serving plate. Spread it thinly with some of the Chocolate Cream Filling and sprinkle it with a few toasted nuts. Top this with a second layer spread with the orange marmalade. Spread the third layer with the Chocolate Cream Filling and the nuts, the fourth with marmalade, the fifth with cream and nuts, and the sixth with the marmalade. Top the cake with the glazed layer and spread the sides with the Chocolate Cream Filling. Decorate the sides of the cake with the remaining toasted Brazil nuts. Chill until 15 minutes prior to serving.

walnut cake

Every collection of dessert recipes should include at least one very special nut cake. . . .

CAKE

Ingredients

1¼ Cups ground walnuts
¾ Cup ground almonds, blanched
2 Cups less 2 tablespoons confectioners' sugar
2 Tablespoons cornstarch
8 Egg whites

Directions

Place the ground nuts, the confectioners' sugar, and the cornstarch in a bowl and mix well. Beat the egg whites until they are stiff. Fold the dry mixture gently into the egg whites. Pour the batter into two buttered and floured 9-inch cake pans. Bake in a slow oven (275 degrees F.) for 1½ to 1¾ hours or until the cakes begin to shrink away from the sides of the pans. Remove the cakes and cool them on a wire rack.

WALNUT CREAM FILLING
Ingredients

1 Cup confectioners' sugar
1 Cup butter
2 Tablespoons Tia Maria coffee liqueur
1 Pinch nutmeg
Rind grated from ½ lemon
1 Cup ground walnuts
3 Drops yellow food coloring

Directions

Sift the confectioners' sugar. Cream the butter and the sifted sugar until light and puffy. Add the remaining ingredients in order, and mix well.

CHOCOLATE ICING
Ingredients

4 Ounces German sweet chocolate
2 Ounces bitter chocolate
3 Tablespoons heavy cream
1 Tablespoon sweet butter
2 Tablespoons confectioners' sugar

Directions

Melt the sweet chocolate and the bitter chocolate in the heavy cream in the top of a double boiler. Beat the butter and confectioners' sugar into the hot chocolate.

TO ASSEMBLE THE CAKE
Ingredients

12 Walnut halves
1 Egg white
¼ Cup coarse sugar

Directions

Place one layer of the cake on a cake plate. Spread this with the Walnut Cream Filling. This layer will be quite thick. Place the remaining walnut layer on top of the Walnut Cream Filling. Ice the cake with the Chocolate Icing. Decorate the top of the cake with walnut halves dipped in egg white and then in coarse sugar.

macaroon
peach
cake

(Serves 10 to 12)

A dream of a dessert is this rich, peachy, coffee cake with macaroon crumbs.

PEACH FILLING
Ingredients

6 Pounds firm, ripe peaches
2 Cups light brown sugar
2 Tablespoons lemon juice
½ Teaspoon nutmeg

Directions

Cover the fruit with scalding water, let stand for five minutes and slip off the skins. Cut the peaches into thick slices and place them in a saucepan. Add the brown sugar, the lemon juice, and the nutmeg, cover, and simmer until the fruit is tender but not mushy. Drain for 2 hours in a colander lined with cheesecloth. Save the juices.

CAKE
Ingredients

1 Cup butter
1 Cup granulated sugar
5 Eggs
1½ Cups finely chopped almonds
1¾ Cups all-purpose flour
1½ Teaspoons baking powder
1½ Teaspoons almond extract
3 Cups *crumbled* almond macaroons (coconut macaroons may be substituted)

Directions

Cream the butter until it is fairly soft. Add the sugar, ¼ cup at a time, beating after each addition. Continue beating until the mixture is light and fluffy. Beat in the eggs, one at a time, beating well after each addition. Fold in the chopped nuts. Sift the flour with the baking powder. Fold this into the batter, along with the almond extract. Butter and flour a 9-inch spring-form pan. Spread half of the batter in the pan and sprinkle with half of the crumbled macaroons. Top these crumbs with half of the drained peaches. Sprinkle the remaining crumbled macaroons over the peaches. Top with the remaining batter.

TOPPING
Ingredients

½ Cup all-purpose flour
½ Cup light brown sugar
¼ Cup chopped almonds
½ Teaspoon cinnamon
4 Tablespoons butter

Directions

Crumble all of the ingredients together with your fingertips. Sprinkle the mixture over the batter and bake for 55 minutes in an oven preheated to 350 degrees F. Cool the cake in the pan.

TO SERVE THE CAKE

Boil the remaining fruit and juices over high heat until the syrup thickens slightly. Remove the cake from the pan, spoon the hot syrup and fruit over it, and top with heavy cream whipped with sugar and nutmeg.

orange nut cake with rum icing

(Serves 10 to 12)

Three layers tall is this old-fashioned Orange Nut Cake. Its rich, buttery flavor is enhanced by candied orange peel, golden raisins, pecans, and a nippy rum icing.

CAKE

Ingredients

⅓ Cup candied orange peel
¾ Cup golden raisins
1 Cup pecans
¾ Cup butter
1½ Cups granulated sugar
3 Eggs

1½ Cups sour milk
3 Cups all-purpose flour
1½ Teaspoons baking soda
¾ Teaspoon salt
3 Tablespoons orange juice
1½ Teaspoons vanilla extract

Directions

Finely chop the candied orange peel and the raisins. Coarsely chop the pecans. Cream the butter until it is soft. Add the sugar, a little at a time, and beat thoroughly. Beat in the eggs, one at a time, and continue to beat for 4 minutes. Sift the flour with the baking soda and the salt. Add the sifted dry ingredients (about ¼ at a time) alternately with the sour milk. Stir in the vanilla, the orange juice, the orange peel, the raisins, and the nuts. Pour the batter into three well-oiled 8-inch round cake pans. Bake for 25 to 30 minutes in an oven preheated to 350 degrees F., or until the cakes pull away from the sides of the pans. Cool.

RUM ICING

Ingredients

3½ Cups confectioners' sugar
½ Cup butter
3 Egg yolks

¼ Teaspoon nutmeg
1 Tablespoon rum

Directions

Cream the sugar and the softened butter. Beat in the egg yolks, the nutmeg, and the rum. Chill.

TO ASSEMBLE THE CAKE

Ingredients

36 Thin strips candied orange peel   12 Unbroken pecan halves

Directions

Turn one of the cooled layers onto a cake plate and ice thinly with the Rum Icing. Top with another layer and spread this with orange marmalade. Top with the third layer and ice the cake with the remaining Rum Icing. Decorate with thin strips of candied orange peel and 12 unbroken halves of pecans.

beer cake

What is the result of mixing conventional cake ingredients with smooth, dark beer? A strange and tangy spice cake. Try it, if you dare!

CAKE
Ingredients

1½ Cups dark beer
(measured after the foam settles)
½ Cup molasses
½ Cup maple syrup
½ Cup butter
1½ Cups raisins
3 Cups all-purpose flour
measured after sifting

1 Teaspoon salt
3 Teaspoons baking powder
½ Teaspoon baking soda
¾ Teaspoon cinnamon
¼ Teaspoon powdered cloves
½ Teaspoon nutmeg
1 Cup coarsely chopped pecans

Directions

In a saucepan, bring the beer, the molasses, the maple syrup, and the butter to a boil and stir until the butter is melted. Remove from the heat and add the raisins. Cool to room temperature.

Sift together the 3 cups of sifted flour, the salt, the baking powder, the baking soda, and the spices. Add this to the beer mixture a little at a time, stirring until smooth. Stir in the chopped pecans, and spoon into a greased and floured tube pan. Bake for 1 hour in an oven preheated to 350 degrees F. Cool.

ICING
Ingredients

1 Cup confectioners' sugar
3 Tablespoons water

1 Egg white
12 Pecan halves

Directions

Mix the confectioners' sugar and the water until smooth. Beat the egg white until it is frothy and add to the sugar mixture. Beat at high speed for several minutes. Ice the top of the cooled cake, allowing the icing to drip over the edges and run down the sides of the cake. Arrange the pecan halves around the top of the cake.

diplomat pudding

Quite delightful is this combination of ladyfingers, vanilla custard, candied citrus peel, and raisins.

VANILLA CUSTARD

Ingredients

3 Cups milk

1 Cup granulated sugar

2-Inch piece of vanilla bean

6 Egg yolks

Directions

Bring the milk, the sugar, and the split vanilla bean to the boiling point in the top of a double boiler but *do not boil*. Stir until the sugar is dissolved. Cool to room temperature. Beat the egg yolks and mix with the sweetened milk. Reserve half of this mixture.

TO ASSEMBLE THE DESSERT

Ingredients

½ Cup apricot jam

3 Packages split ladyfingers (approximately 50 whole sponge fingers)

¼ Cup chopped citron

½ Cup sliced candied cherries

2 Tablespoons chopped orange peel

½ Cup golden raisins

½ Cup dark raisins

¼ Cup Cointreau

Directions

Spread the bottom of an assembled 9-inch spring-form pan with apricot jam. Arrange a layer of *split* ladyfingers attractively on the jam and sprinkle them with small amounts of chopped citron, sliced cherries, chopped orange peel, raisins, and Cointreau. Spoon a little Vanilla Custard over this and repeat the process until all of the ladyfingers, fruit, and Cointreau and *half* of the Vanilla Custard have been used. Cover the bottom and sides of the pan with several wrappings of aluminum foil and bake for 1 hour in an oven preheated to 325 degrees F.

Cook the remaining Vanilla Custard over boiling water, stirring constantly, until it coats a silver spoon. Remove the vanilla bean and chill the custard, stirring occasionally.

Remove the Diplomat Pudding from the oven, invert onto a serving plate, decorate with candied fruit, and serve with the chilled Vanilla Custard in a separate dish.

pêches melba

Why not try this easy-to-prepare treat for those special guests?

POACHED PEACHES
Ingredients

6 Fully ripe peaches
1½ Cups water
1½ Cups granulated sugar

2-Inch piece of vanilla bean
2 Teaspoons lemon juice

Directions

Place the peaches in a Pyrex bowl. Cover with boiling water. Lift out one peach, cut it in half, and carefully remove the pit. Gently pull off the skin with a paring knife. Repeat the process with the remaining peaches. Place 1½ cups of boiling water, the sugar, and the split vanilla bean in a saucepan. Bring to a boil over a high flame. Add the peach halves and lemon juice, and boil for 3 minutes. Chill the peaches in the syrup.

RASPBERRY SYRUP
Ingredients

2 Cups thawed frozen
   raspberries in their syrup
1 Cup seedless raspberry jelly

3 Tablespoons cornstarch
3 Tablespoons cold water
1 Tablespoon lemon juice

Directions

Combine the raspberries in their syrup, the sugar, and the raspberry jelly in a saucepan and stir until fairly well mixed. Mix the cornstarch, the cold water, and the lemon juice to a smooth paste, and stir into the raspberry mixture. Cook, stirring constantly until the sauce is thick and clear. Strain and chill.

TO SERVE
Ingredients

12 Scoops vanilla ice cream

Directions

Place a scoop of vanilla ice cream in each of twelve silver or crystal bowls. Top each with one well-drained peach half, rounded side up. Spoon the Raspberry Syrup over the peaches and serve immediately.

biscuit tortoni

(Serves 10 to 12)

This might be just the dessert to serve when your dinner guests include children. It is easy to prepare and simply yummy.

Ingredients

2 Cups heavy cream
1 Cup confectioners' sugar
2 Egg whites
½ Teaspoon almond extract
¾ Cup fine almond macaroon crumbs

Directions

Beat the cream until it has thickened somewhat but is not stiff. Continue beating while you sprinkle in the sugar. Beat the egg whites until they stand in stiff peaks and fold them, along with the almond extract, into the sweetened whipped cream. Spoon the mixture into twelve small individual paper cups or soufflé dishes and sprinkle each with macaroon crumbs. Cover with aluminum foil and freeze for 3 hours. Serve frozen.

coconut
charlotte
russe
with
two sauces

(Serves 10 to 12)

Here's a sweet that is as white, as light, and as fluffy as a Russian hat. It sports two sauces, side by side: one cara-mel, one chocolate—both delicious.

COCONUT CHOCOLATE RUSSE
Ingredients

1½ Tablespoons unflavored gelatin
3 Tablespoons water
1 Cup light cream
¾ Cup granulated sugar
1½ Cups heavy cream
2 Egg whites
2 Cups finely grated coconut
1 Teaspoon almond extract

Directions

Measure the gelatin and sprinkle it over the water to soften. Scald the light cream. Stir the gelatin and ¼ cup of sugar into the hot cream until both are dissolved. Bring this mixture to room tem-perature and then chill it in the freezer (or refrigerator), stirring frequently until it begins to thicken. Meanwhile, whip the heavy cream. Reserve. Beat the egg whites until they are fairly stiff. Add

½ cup of sugar a little at a time and continue to beat until the egg whites hold a peak. Fold the whipped cream, the egg whites, the coconut, and the almond extract into the slightly thickened gelatin mixture. Carefully spoon the mixture into a charlotte mold or an attractively shaped dish. Chill for several hours or until firm. Unmold onto a cold platter. Decorate with alternate stripes of Chocolate Sauce and Caramel Cream Sauce. Serve very cold.

CHOCOLATE SAUCE
Ingredients

2 Squares bitter chocolate	½ Cup light cream
1 Tablespoon butter	½ Teaspoon vanilla
½ Cup granulated sugar	

Directions

Place the chocolate squares and the butter in a small heavy skillet or in the top of a double boiler. Melt the chocolate over low heat. In a mixing bowl combine the sugar and the cream. Add to the melted chocolate. Stir over a medium-low flame until the sauce reaches the boiling point. Reduce heat. Cook over a low flame until the sauce thickens slightly. Stir in the vanilla. Cool.

CARAMEL CREAM SAUCE
Ingredients

1 Tablespoon apple juice (or liquid from canned peaches or pears)
¾ Cup granulated sugar
8 Teaspoons butter
½ Cup heavy cream

Directions

Heat the oven to its hottest temperature. Sprinkle sugar in the bottom of a baking dish. Sprinkle the sugar with the fruit juice and dot with the teaspoons of butter. Place the sugar in the dish on the center shelf of the oven and allow the sugar to turn brown. Stir occasionally. Remove the dish from the oven and stir the heavy cream into the caramelized sugar in the dish. Cool. To serve, dribble alternate stripes of cool Chocolate Sauce and Caramel Cream Sauce over the cold Coconut Charlotte Russe. For a more dramatic effect allow some of the white Coconut Charlotte Russe to show between the stripes of sauce. Serve very cold with extra sauce in separate dishes.

mont-blanc
aux marrons

(Serves 10 to 12)

This is an outstanding dessert, but one that shouldn't be prepared when you are in a hurry. The cooked chestnuts must be rubbed through a fine sieve until not a single lump remains to clog the smallest nozzle of a pastry bag. The chestnut purée is then piped into a ring and filled with sweetened whipped cream.

Ingredients

1½ Pounds fine chestnuts	2 Tablespoons Cointreau
3 Cups milk	6 Tablespoons water
2-Inch piece of vanilla bean	2-Inch piece of vanilla bean
1 Cup granulated sugar	3 Tablespoons sweet butter

Directions

Use a sharp knife to cut a slit around each chestnut. Cover the chestnuts with cold water and boil for 5 minutes. Do not drain the chestnuts, but pluck them one at a time from the hot water, quickly remove the shell, and brown the inner skin. Reheat the water if the skins become difficult to remove. Place the peeled chestnuts in a pan of the milk scalded with one piece of the vanilla bean. Bring the chestnuts and the milk to a boil, lower the flame, and simmer until the chestnuts are soft *throughout*. Drain off and discard the milk. Rub the chestnuts through a sieve. Place the chestnuts and the Cointreau in the container of a blender, and blend at a high speed until the purée is very smooth.

Bring the sugar, the water, and the remaining piece of vanilla bean to a boil in a heavy saucepan. Cook until the syrup forms a soft ball when a little is dropped into a cup of cold water. Discard the vanilla bean. Mix the chestnut purée and the syrup, working it well until it becomes a thick paste. Strain again. When the paste is nearly cool, stir in the butter.

Fill a pastry bag with the chestnut paste and force it through a small, round tube into a buttered, sugared ring mold. Cross and crisscross the strands of the chestnut paste to obtain a nestlike effect. While the purée is still warm, carefully unmold it onto a chilled serving platter. Chill for 2 hours. Just prior to serving, fill with chilled whipped cream.

WHIPPED CREAM
Ingredients

1½ Cups heavy cream
5 Tablespoons granulated sugar
1 Teaspoon vanilla

Directions

Whip the cream until it begins to thicken, and continue beating while you sprinkle in the sugar. Beat until the cream holds a peak. Fold in the vanilla extract. Chill until time to serve.

cromquemboche

Imagine a little Christmas tree made of sweet, golden cream puffs dipped in caramel and set one on top of the other. This attractive and unusual dessert will long be remembered by friends and family.

PÂTE À CHOUX
Ingredients

1 Cup water

½ Cup butter

1¼ Cups all-purpose flour

5 Eggs

Directions

Boil the water and the butter together in a pan. Add the flour all at one time, and stir rapidly with a wooden spoon until the dough leaves the sides of the pan and forms a ball. Remove the pan from the heat and beat in the eggs, one at a time, beating after each addition. Continue beating until the mixture is smooth and has a sheen. Use two spoons to drop small amounts (about the size of a walnut) of Pâte à Choux onto a buttered cookie sheet. Bake for 15 minutes at 425 degrees F.; then lower the heat to 375 degrees F. and bake until the puffs are light golden brown (approximately 15 to 20 minutes). Remove from the oven and set aside to cool.

TART PASTRY
Ingredients

1 Cup presifted all-purpose flour

¼ Teaspoon salt

½ Cup butter

3 or 4 Tablespoons ice water

Directions

Sift the flour and the salt into a mixing bowl. Cut in the butter with a pastry blender or two knives until the mixture has the consistency of corn meal. Add the remaining butter and blend until the particles are the size of small peas. Sprinkle in the ice water and stir with a fork until the pastry forms a ball. Refrigerate for 10 minutes. Roll out the pastry on a lightly floured surface to a circle 9 inches in diameter. Press this into the bottom of a 9-inch spring-form pan. Bake at 450 degrees F. for 10 to 15 minutes or until golden. Remove from the oven and allow to cool.

PASTRY CREAM

Ingredients

⅓ Cup granulated sugar	2 Cups milk
4 Tablespoons cornstarch	2-Inch piece of vanilla bean (or 1 tea-
6 Egg yolks	spoon extract of vanilla)

Directions

Place the sugar, the cornstarch, and the egg yolks in the top of a double boiler. Mix well. Use another saucepan to scald the milk. Slit the vanilla bean and stir it into the milk. (If vanilla extract is used, it must be added after the Pastry Cream is chilled.) Pour the scalded milk, with the vanilla bean, slowly over the egg-yolk mixture, stirring rapidly. Cook the mixture over boiling water, stirring constantly, until it is quite thick. Do not allow the cream to boil or it will curdle. Remove the vanilla bean and strain the cream into the ovenproof bowl. Chill, stirring occasionally to prevent a skin from forming on top of the cream. Use a pastry tube with a rather wide nozzle to fill the cream puffs without removing their tops.

CARAMEL SYRUP

Ingredients

1½ Cups granulated sugar	1 Cup water

Directions

Mix the sugar and water in a large pan and boil, stirring constantly until the syrup turns a golden brown. Do not allow the syrup to become too dark. Remove from the heat and use immediately.

TO ASSEMBLE

Place the pastry crust on a serving plate. Use a pair of tongs to dip the cream puffs carefully into the *hot* Caramel Syrup (reheat the syrup if necessary), and arrange them on the pastry crust, building them into a Christmas tree shape. The sticky Caramel Syrup will hold the puffs in place as it cools. Be careful not to allow the Caramel Syrup to touch your hands, since it gives a nasty burn.

steamed
chocolate
pudding

(Serves 10 to 12)

A nice variation for Christmas dinner—a steamed choco-late pudding decorated with red and green candied cherries.

PUDDING
Ingredients

¾ Cup butter
9 Slices rich white bread
1 Cup less 2 tablespoons heavy cream
9 Eggs
4 Egg yolks
¾ Cup ground blanched almonds
4 Ounces bittersweet chocolate
1 Cup granulated sugar

Directions

Cream the butter in a large mixing bowl. Soak the bread in the heavy cream for 10 minutes. Beat the bread, and cream it into the butter. Add the eggs and the egg yolks and continue beating until thoroughly mixed. Grind the almonds. Melt the chocolate in the top of a double boiler over boiling water. Add the ground nuts, the melted chocolate, and the sugar to the egg yolk mixture. Beat well. Butter a tall two-quart mold or steamed pudding mold and pour in the pudding mixture. Tie a double thickness of aluminum foil over the top to seal the mold and place it in a kettle of boiling water. The water should come three-fourths of the way up the mold. Steam the pudding for 1½ hours or until the pudding is firm to the touch. If necessary, add more boiling water to keep the water level constant. Unmold the pudding onto a serving plate.

TOPPING
Ingredients

2 Cups heavy cream
½ Cup granulated sugar

1 Tablespoon rum
10 Candied cherries

Directions

Whip the cream until it begins to thicken. Add the sugar gradually and continue beating until the cream is fairly thick. Sprinkle the rum over the whipped cream and beat for a few seconds more. Pipe 10 rosettes of whipped cream around the bottom of the steamed pudding. Place a candied cherry in the center of each rosette. To achieve a seasonal, festive look at Christmas time, alternate red and green cherries.

oeufs à la neige
(snow eggs)

(Serves 10 to 12)

This dessert is so named because of the egg-shaped meringue puffs that delicately float on a small, creamy sea of custard sauce. The custard complements the sweet, ripe strawberry slices that line the bottom of the glass serving bowl. If you like Strawberry Trifle, you'll probably love this.

MERINGUE

Ingredients

5 Egg whites

⅞ Cup granulated sugar

Milk for poaching the snow eggs

Directions

Beat the egg whites until they are fairly stiff and continue beating as you gradually add the sugar. Beat for 2 minutes more. Pour milk into a 5- or 6-inch pan until the liquid is two inches deep. Simmer the milk over a *very low* flame. Use two wet tablespoons to form the meringue into egg shapes. Slip the meringues into the simmering milk and poach them for 3 or 4 minutes on each side. (Don't be lazy. Rinse the spoons after you form each "egg.") Use a slotted spoon to remove the snow eggs from the milk and drain them on absorbent paper.

CUSTARD SAUCE
Ingredients

1½ Cups cream
1½ Cups milk
3-Inch piece of vanilla bean (or
1¼ teaspoons vanilla extract)
8 Egg yolks
¾ Cup granulated sugar

Directions

Scald the cream and the milk with the split piece of vanilla bean. (If vanilla extract is used, it must be added after the custard is cool.) Place the egg yolks and sugar in the top of a double boiler and beat until they are light and creamy. Gradually beat the hot cream and milk into the egg yolk mixture. Cook in the top of a double boiler over gently boiling water, stirring constantly until the custard thickens enough to cover a spoon. Strain the sauce and chill it, stirring occasionally.

STRAWBERRIES
Ingredients

8 Cups fresh strawberries

Directions

Wash, hull, and slice the strawberries. Place them in a large, deep, glass bowl and chill.

TO ASSEMBLE
Ingredients

½ Cup toasted, slivered almonds

Directions

Pour the cold Custard Sauce over the chilled strawberries. Place the snow eggs on top and sprinkle with toasted, slivered almonds. Serve cold.

crème de menthe pie

Mint-cool and creamy is this interesting pie.

CRUST

Ingredients

1¾ Cups crushed chocolate cookies filled with mint-flavored cream
¼ Cup melted sweet butter

Directions

Be sure the mint-filled chocolate cookies are crushed to fine crumbs. Stir in the melted butter. Mix well. Press the mixture into the bottom of an assembled 9-inch spring-form pan. Bake for 5 minutes in an oven preheated to 450 degrees F. Cool in the pan.

FILLING

Ingredients

2 Tablespoons unflavored gelatin
1 Cup heavy cream
8 Egg yolks
½ Cup granulated sugar

⅓ Cup green crème de menthe
⅓ Cup white crème de cacao
1½ Cups heavy cream

Directions

Soften the gelatin in 1 cup of heavy cream in the top of a double boiler. Heat the mixture until the gelatin is dissolved. Cool slightly and beat in the egg yolks and the sugar. Stir in the crème de menthe and the crème de cacao. Chill until the mixture begins to thicken. Meanwhile whip 1½ cups of heavy cream until it is stiff, reserve ¼ cup of whipped cream, and fold the remainder into the slightly thickened gelatin mixture. Spread the filling over the cooled cookie crust and chill until the pie is firm. To serve, decorate with small mint-flavored chocolates and the reserved whipped cream piped through a decorative nozzle of a pastry tube.

strawberries romanoff

(Serves 10 to 12)

Simply *delicious!*

Ingredients

3 Quarts strawberries
1¼ Cups granulated sugar
1 Cup freshly squeezed, strained
   orange juice
¾ Cup Cointreau
3 Cups heavy cream
8 Tablespoons granulated sugar
3 Tablespoons Cointreau

Directions

Wash the berries if they are sandy, and drain them thoroughly. Remove the hulls and place the strawberries in a large bowl. Mix 1¼ cups of sugar, the orange juice, and ¾ cup of Cointreau. Pour the mixture over the berries and chill for at least an hour. Beat the cream until it is slightly thickened and continue to beat while you sprinkle in 8 tablespoons of sugar. Beat the cream until it is quite stiff and fold in 3 tablespoons of Cointreau. To serve, place the berries and the liquid in a large glass bowl. Use a pastry tube fitted with a fluted nozzle to pipe points of whipped cream over them.

little somethings

éclairs

(Serves 10 to 12)

One of the most popular desserts I can think of is the chocolate éclair. It seems to disappear like magic from any dessert plate. Strong indeed is the guest who doesn't come back for another of these easy-to-make yet impressive sweets.

PÂTE À CHOUX

Ingredients

1 Cup water
½ Cup butter

1¼ Cups all-purpose flour
5 Eggs

Directions

Boil the water and the butter together in a saucepan. Add the flour all at one time, and stir rapidly with a wooden spoon until the dough leaves the sides of the pan and forms a ball. Remove the pan from the heat and beat in the eggs, one at a time, beating after each addition. Continue beating until the mixture is smooth and has a sheen. Pipe the Pâte à Choux through a pastry tube (with no nozzle) onto a buttered cookie sheet. Bake for 15 minutes at 425 degrees F. and then lower the heat to 375 degrees F., and bake until the éclairs are light golden brown (approximately 15 minutes), or until the sides feel rigid. Do not allow the éclairs to become too brown. Remove from the oven and set aside to cool.

PASTRY CREAM
Ingredients

⅓ Cup granulated sugar
4 Tablespoons cornstarch
6 Egg yolks
2 Cups milk
2-Inch piece of vanilla bean (or 1 teaspoon extract of vanilla)

Directions

Place the sugar, the cornstarch, and the egg yolks in the top of a double boiler. Mix well. Use another saucepan to scald the milk. Slit the vanilla bean and stir it into the milk (if vanilla extract is used, it must be added after the pastry cream is chilled). Stir rapidly while slowly pouring the scalded milk, with the vanilla bean, over the egg yolk mixture. Cook the mixture over boiling water, stirring constantly until it is quite thick. Remove the vanilla bean and strain the cream into an ovenproof bowl. Chill, stirring occasionally to prevent a skin from forming on top of the cream. Use a pastry tube with a rather wide nozzle to fill the éclairs, or split and fill. Set aside.

CHOCOLATE FROSTING
Ingredients

1 Ounce cream cheese
¾ Cup confectioners' sugar
1 Square unsweetened chocolate

1 Pinch salt
Heavy sweet cream

Directions

Cream the cheese until it is fluffy. Add the sugar a little at a time, mixing after each addition. Melt the chocolate over boiling water and stir it, with the salt, into the cheese mixture. Add just enough heavy cream to make the icing spread nicely. Spread the icing along the top of the éclair.

little somethings

cream
puffs

(Serves 10 to 12)

The cream puff is a dessert favorite of millions. You'll never go wrong when you decide to serve a plate of these delicate and delicious treats.

PÂTE À CHOUX
Ingredients

1 Cup water
½ Cup butter
1¼ Cups all-purpose flour
5 Eggs

Directions

Boil the water and the butter together in a saucepan. Add the flour, all at one time, and stir rapidly with a wooden spoon until the dough leaves the sides of the pan and forms a ball. Remove the pan from the heat and beat in the eggs, one at a time, beating after each addition. Continue beating until the mixture is smooth and has a sheen. Drop spoonfuls of Pâte à Choux onto a buttered cookie sheet. Bake for 15 minutes at 425 degrees F. and then lower the heat to 375 degrees F. and bake until the puffs are light golden brown (approximately 15 to 18 minutes), or until the sides of the puffs feel rigid. Do not allow the puffs to become too brown. Remove from the oven and set aside to cool.

PASTRY CREAM
Ingredients

⅓ Cup granulated sugar
4 Tablespoons cornstarch
6 Egg yolks
2 Cups milk
2-Inch piece of vanilla bean (or 1 teaspoon extract of vanilla)

Directions

Place the sugar, the cornstarch, and the egg yolks in the top of a double boiler. Mix well. Use another saucepan to scald the milk. Slit the vanilla bean and stir it into the milk. (If vanilla extract is used, it must be added after the pastry cream is chilled.) Pour the scalded milk, with the vanilla bean, slowly into the egg yolk mixture, stirring rapidly. Cook the mixture over boiling water, stirring constantly, until the cream is quite thick. Remove the vanilla bean and strain the cream into an ovenproof bowl. Chill, stirring occasionally to prevent a skin from forming on top of the cream. Use a pastry tube with a rather wide nozzle to fill the cream puffs without removing their tops, or cut a cap off the top of each puff, fill it with cream, and replace the cap. Sprinkle with confectioners' sugar.

little somethings

danish pastry*

(Makes about 2 dozen pastries—serves 10 to 12)

Danish pastries, filled with poppy seed, pineapple, apricot, or cherry—take your pick. A tasty assortment for a company breakfast, brunch, or late-night snack.

PASTRY

Ingredients

¾ Pound sweet butter
4 Cups all-purpose flour
1½ Packages dry yeast

1¼ Cups milk
1 Egg
¼ Cup granulated sugar

Directions

Chill the butter, place it in a mixing bowl, and sift ⅓ cup of flour over it. Use a pastry blender or two knives to cut the butter and the flour into a coarse meal. Chill the mixture and then roll it between two sheets of waxed paper into a rectangle about 6 by 12 inches. Chill this sheet in the refrigerator while you prepare the following:

Heat the milk to lukewarm (no warmer). Place it in a rather large bowl and sprinkle the yeast over it. Let stand until the yeast is moist and softened and the milk has cooled. Beat the egg and add it, with the sugar, to the yeast. Sift the remainder of the flour and use a wooden spoon to gradually beat it into the egg-milk-yeast mixture to form a soft dough. If this dough seems a bit too sticky to handle, add a little more flour. Turn the dough onto a floured surface and knead it until it is smooth and has a slight gloss. Roll out the dough to form a rectangle 7 by 14 inches.

* Prepare on a cool day or in an air-conditioned kitchen.

Remove the butter dough from the refrigerator and place it over half of the rolled yeast dough. Fold over the other half of the yeast dough quickly and lightly with your hands and then roll it out into a large rectangle about ¼ to ½ inch thick. Fold this sheet of dough into thirds to make three layers. Chill the dough for 20 minutes and then roll it out again to a large rectangle ¼ to ½ inch thick. Fold the dough into thirds and roll it out. Fold it as before, chill it for 20 minutes, and roll it out. At this point the dough may be chilled either for 20 minutes or overnight, and then rolled out and cut into triangles, squares, or rectangles. These are to be filled and formed into envelopes, cockscombs, or what my grandmother called "cradles," where the dough is folded across the center of the filling like a little blanket.

POPPY SEED FILLING
Ingredients

½ Cup poppy seeds
6 Tablespoons granulated sugar

¼ Cup milk
1 Tablespoon lemon juice

Directions

Whirl the poppy seeds in a blender for a few minutes, stopping the machine several times to stir the uncracked seeds to the top. Place this poppy seed powder in a small saucepan with the sugar and the milk, and stir constantly over a low heat for 5 minutes. Add the lemon juice and cook for 1 minute more, or until the mixture is very thick. Cool.

APRICOT FILLING
Ingredients

1 Cup dried apricots
1 Cup granulated sugar

1 Cup water

Directions

Boil the above ingredients, stirring from time to time until the apricots are tender and the syrup is very thick. Cool.

CHERRY FILLING
Ingredients

1 Cup canned pitted sour cherries, drained (reserve liquid)
1 Cup granulated sugar

½ Cup cherry juice
⅛ Teaspoon nutmeg
¼ Teaspoon cinnamon

Directions

Boil the above ingredients until the syrup is very thick. Cool.

PINEAPPLE FILLING

Ingredients

1 Cup fresh pineapple (peeled, cored, and chopped)
¼ Cup canned or fresh pineapple juice
1 Cup granulated sugar

Directions

Peel, core, and chop the pineapple. Cook the pineapple, the pineapple juice, and the sugar over a low heat for 10 minutes, or until the mixture is very thick. Cool.

TO ASSEMBLE THE PASTRIES

Roll out the prepared, chilled dough to a sheet about ¼ inch thick. Cut one large piece of dough about 5 inches wide and 12 inches long. Place the Poppy Seed Filling down the center of the dough, fold the dough over, and press the ends together. Cut into 4 lengths to form four 3-inch cockscombs. Slice through the pressed edges of the dough at ¾-inch intervals. Do not cut into the filling. Bend the pastries slightly to resemble cockscombs.

Cut the remaining dough into 4-inch squares. Place 1 tablespoon of the desired filling in the center of each square, bend in the corners, and press down lightly.

Spread the remaining squares with filling to within one-half inch of the edges of the dough. Fold two opposite corners of the dough across the filling and press them together lightly (but be sure they hold). This will form a small "cradle" with a "blanket" tucked across the middle and the filling showing at either end. Bend the edges of this dough up *slightly* around the filling, retaining the points on either end.

Place the pastries on a lightly greased baking sheet, cover them with a cloth, and set them to rise in a warm place (free from drafts) until they are half doubled in size.

When they have risen properly, brush each with beaten egg diluted with a little water. Bake about 15 minutes (or until brown) in an oven preheated to 400 degrees F. Cool on racks.

desserts
to serve
twelve to sixteen
persons

An exciting prospect, indeed, is the gathering together of this many friends or acquaintances (or even enemies for that matter). A dessert must make more than a quiet statement if it is to be noticed amid the animated conversation that is sure to ensue.

I promise you that no matter how great the conversational pyrotechnics, the following desserts will not pass unnoticed.

raisin-cheese pie

(Serves 12 to 16)

One of the richest of the super-rich desserts is this raisin pie with kuchen crust and cheesecake topping. No one who loves desserts should miss this.

KUCHEN DOUGH
Ingredients

1 Cup all-purpose flour   ½ Cup butter
2½ Tablespoons granulated sugar   1 Egg yolk
⅛ Teaspoon salt

Directions

Sift the dry ingredients together. Cut in the butter with a pastry cutter or two knives to produce a mealy mixture. Lightly beat the egg yolk in a cup and use a fork to stir it into the flour-butter mixture. With the back of a spoon press the dough evenly into the bottom of an assembled spring-form pan. Set the pan on a middle rack and bake at 350 degrees F. for 30 minutes. Remove from the oven and set on a wire rack. Cool in the pan.

FRUIT FILLING
Ingredients

2 Cups coarsely chopped raisins   4 Tablespoons cornstarch
2 Cups peeled chopped fresh   ¼ Teaspoon salt
     peaches   ¼ Teaspoon nutmeg
½ Cup granulated sugar   1 Teaspoon red wine vinegar
3 Tablespoons Grand Marnier   1 Teaspoon butter
1 Cup water

Directions

Chop the raisins. Peel, pit, and chop fresh, ripe peaches. Combine the fruit, the sugar, and the Grand Marnier in a saucepan. Mix the water, the cornstarch, the salt, and the nutmeg. Add this mixture to the fruit in the saucepan, and stir over medium heat until it bubbles and turns clear and thick. Remove the pan from the flame and stir in the vinegar and the butter. Cool.

CHEESE TOPPING
Ingredients

8 Ounces cream cheese	1 Pinch salt
½ Vanilla bean, split in half lengthwise	1 Egg
	¼ Cup granulated sugar

Directions

Beat the cream cheese in a small bowl until it is light and puffy. Add the salt. Scrape the tiny seeds from the split vanilla bean and stir these into the cheese. Beat the egg and sugar for several minutes, or until the mixture is smooth and light yellow in color. Beat this into the cheese mixture, pausing several times to scrape the bottom of the bowl. Spread the cooled fruit filling evenly over the kuchen pastry. Smooth the cheese topping over the fruit filling and bake at 350 degrees F. for 40 minutes. Remove from the oven and place on a wire rack to cool.

WALNUT STREUSEL TOPPING
Ingredients

3 Tablespoons finely chopped walnuts	6 Tablespoons light brown sugar
3 Tablespoons all-purpose flour	¼ Cup butter

Directions

Chop the walnuts until they are quite fine. (The nuts *may* be ground, but grinding produces pieces of nut with round or crushed edges. Chopping the nuts gives them sharp edges and results in a crunchier topping.) Mix chopped nuts, flour, and brown sugar in a mixing bowl. Cut in the butter with a pastry cutter or two knives until the mixture is reduced to coarse crumbs. Sprinkle these crumbs over the cheese topping and broil (at about 5 inches from the flame) until the crumbs are lightly browned (be sure to watch over this process carefully; this streusel topping burns easily). Remove from the broiler and cool. Serve freshly baked at room temperature or chilled.

old german
poppy seed
cheesecake

(Serves 12 to 16)

My grandfather, Nicholas Young, was a fine, kind man and, among other things, a talented baker. I truly believe his recipe for cheesecake with poppy seed topping is one of the best in the world.

BOTTOM CRUST
Ingredients

1 Cup all-purpose flour	¼ Teaspoon salt
2½ Tablespoons granulated sugar	7 Tablespoons butter
1 Tablespoon confectioners' sugar	1 Large egg yolk

Directions

Sift the dry ingredients together, cut in the butter, and stir in the egg yolk. Mix well. Assemble a 9-inch spring-form pan, and use your fingers to press the dough over the bottom. Bake 20 minutes in an oven preheated to 350 degrees F. Cool in the pan.

CHEESE FILLING
Ingredients

28 Ounces cream cheese	⅓ Teaspoon salt
3 Eggs	1 Vanilla bean
¾ Cup granulated sugar	

Directions

Work the cream cheese with a spoon or cream it in an electric beater until it is very soft and smooth. Add the eggs, one at a time, beating until smooth after each addition. Continue beating while you sprinkle in the sugar. Split the vanilla bean, scrape out the seeds and add them, with the salt, to the cream cheese mixture. Beat for 5 minutes, stopping several times to scrape the bottom of the bowl. Pour this batter over the cooled crust. Bake for 1 hour in an oven preheated to 350 degrees F. Cool the cake in the pan on a wire rack.

POPPY-SEED TOPPING
Ingredients

1½ Cups crushed poppy seeds
¼ Cup water
1 Cup dark raisins
1 Cup granulated sugar

½ Cup milk
½ Teaspoon vanilla extract
1 Lemon

Directions

Pound the poppy seeds in a mortar with a pestle (or whirl in a blender) until they are crushed and resemble a dark gray powder. Place the water and raisins in a saucepan and cook over a medium flame until the water evaporates. Add the crushed poppy seeds, the sugar, and the milk, and cook over a low flame, stirring constantly for 15 or 20 minutes or until the mixture is very thick. Cool and beat in the juice of the lemon and the vanilla extract. Spread over the cooled cake. Do not remove the cake from the pan.

NUT TOPPING
Ingredients

½ Cup light brown sugar
½ Cup all-purpose flour
½ Cup finely chopped walnuts
½ Cup butter

Directions

Mix the brown sugar, the flour, and the chopped walnuts. Cut in the butter until all the ingredients are the coarseness of the chopped nuts. Sprinkle over the cake and place under the broiler until lightly browned. Watch this process closely as the nut topping burns easily. Serve cold or at room temperature.

orange glazed cheesecake

(Serves 12 to 16)

This cheesecake is different! Its crust is crunchy, it has a creamy sour cream topping, a clear sparkling orange glaze, and *it's decorated with slices of candied orange and nuts.*

CRUST
Ingredients

1½ Cups zwieback crumbs
½ Cup melted butter
6 Tablespoons granulated sugar
7 Tablespoons ground unblanched almonds
2 Tablespoons heavy cream

Directions

Crush the zwieback with a rolling pin and place the crumbs in a large mixing bowl. Melt the butter and stir it into the crumbs. Add the sugar and the ground almonds and mix well. Stir in the heavy cream and press the crumbs firmly against the bottom of a 9-inch spring-form pan. Bake for 15 minutes in an oven pre-heated to 375 degrees F. Cool the crust at room temperature. Chill.

CHEESE FILLING
Ingredients

4 Eight-ounce packages cream cheese
1 Cup granulated sugar
1 Tablespoon Cointreau
3 Tablespoons cognac
4 Drops orange flavoring
4-Inch piece of vanilla bean or 2 teaspoons vanilla
4 Eggs

Directions

In the large bowl of your electric mixer, beat the cream cheese until it is soft and puffy. Add the sugar, the Cointreau, the cognac, and the orange flavoring. Split the vanilla bean and scrape out the soft inside. Stir this into the cream cheese mixture. Beat for 5 minutes, stopping frequently to scrape bottom and sides of mixing bowl. Separate the egg whites from the yolks. Add the egg yolks, one at a time, to the cheese mixture, beating well after each addition. Beat the egg whites until they are stiff but not dry. Fold these into the cheese mixture. Spoon over the chilled crust. Bake for 1 hour in an oven preheated to 300 degrees F.

TOPPING
Ingredients

1 Cup sour cream
1 Tablespoon granulated sugar
1 Teaspoon vanilla

Directions

Mix ingredients thoroughly. Spread over the top of the hot cake. Bake 10 minutes at 300 degrees F.

ORANGE GLAZE
Ingredients

1 Cup granulated sugar
1 Cup orange juice
18 Very thin strips of peel with white pith removed
2 Tablespoons cornstarch
¼ Cup water
15 Whole almonds

Directions

Bring the sugar, orange juice, and orange peel to a boil. Mix cornstarch and water until it is a smooth paste. Add this to the orange juice and boil, stirring constantly, until the glaze is clear and thick. Cool slightly. Spread over the top of the cheesecake. To decorate: Use the glazed orange peel and whole almonds to form almond flowers with orange peel stems.

chocolate fruit and nut cake

(Serves 12 to 16)

Almost too easy to believe is the recipe for this chewy cake made with whole nuts and candied fruits. Bake at Christmas time, wrap attractively, and give to friends. You'll be the most popular Santa you know.

Ingredients

¾ Cup shelled pistachio nuts
¾ Cup blanched almonds
1 Cup pecan halves
3 Tablespoons cocoa
1½ Teaspoons cinnamon
¼ Teaspoon nutmeg
¼ Teaspoon allspice

½ Cup all-purpose flour
½ Cup red candied cherries
½ Cup green candied cherries
¾ Cup candied orange peel
¾ Cup granulated sugar
¾ Cup honey

Directions

Mix the pistachio nuts, the blanched almonds, the pecan halves, the cocoa, the cinnamon, the nutmeg, the allspice, the flour, and the candied fruit. Place the sugar and the honey in a large saucepan, bring them to a boil, and then simmer until a little of the syrup dropped in cold water forms a *soft* ball, or a candy thermometer registers 238 degrees F. Remove from the heat and stir in the fruit mixture. Mix thoroughly. Line a 9-inch spring-form pan with buttered paper and turn the fruit and nut mixture into it. Bake the cake for 30 minutes in an oven preheated to 300 degrees F. Cool the cake before removing it from the pan. Serve at room temperature.

TOPPING

Ingredients

1 Cup semi-sweet chocolate bits
1 Tablespoon dark rum
½ Tablespoon butter

Directions

Place the chocolate bits, the rum, and the butter in the top of a double boiler. Melt over boiling water. Stir for 4 minutes. Dribble the chocolate mixture over the cooled cake.

ginger cheesecake

(Serves 12 to 16)

The addition of exotic candied ginger gives this moist cheesecake a unique and subtle flavor.

CRUST

Ingredients

1 Box (6 ounces) zwieback, ground
1 Cup granulated sugar
1 Cup finely chopped walnuts
¾ Cup finely chopped candied ginger

¼ Teaspoon powdered ginger
¼ Teaspoon cinnamon
⅔ Cup melted butter

Directions

With your fingers, crumble together the *ground* zwieback, the sugar, the chopped nuts, the chopped candied ginger, the powdered ginger, and the cinnamon. Stir in the melted butter and mix thoroughly. Press half of these buttered crumbs* into the greased bottom of an assembled 9-inch spring-form pan. Bake for 10 minutes in an oven preheated to 325 degrees F. Cool in the pan.

CHEESECAKE

Ingredients

2 Pounds pot cheese
5 Eggs
1¼ Cups granulated sugar
½ Pint sweet cream
8 Ounces cream cheese
¼ Cup all-purpose flour

½ Cup sweetened condensed milk
Grated yellow outer rind from
  1 lemon
3 Tablespoons lemon juice
¼ Teaspoon salt
¼ Teaspoon powdered ginger

Directions

Rub the pot cheese twice through a fine sieve. In a large bowl, beat the eggs and sugar until they are light in color. Add the sieved pot cheese and the remaining ingredients, beating after each addition. Pour onto the baked, cooled zwieback crust. Sprinkle the cheesecake mixture with the remaining crumb mixture, and bake for 1¼ hours in an oven preheated to 350 degrees F. Allow the cake to remain in the hot oven for 1 hour after the heat has been turned off. Cool and then chill. Serve cold.

* Reserve the remaining crumbs to use as a topping.

old-fashioned
chocolate
icebox
cake

(Serves 12 to 16)

Here's an icebox cake just like grandma used to make. Macaroons, bittersweet chocolate icing, ladyfingers, and rich chocolate pudding nestle layer on layer to form this old-fashioned sweet.

Ingredients

3 Tablespoons heavy cream
4 Ounces German sweet chocolate
2 Ounces bitter chocolate
2 Tablespoons confectioners' sugar
1 Tablespoon sweet butter
½ Cup granulated sugar
4 Egg yolks
1 Cup milk
1 Teaspoon vanilla extract
3 Dozen ladyfingers
¼ Cup cream sherry
1½ Dozen almond macaroons (coconut macaroons may be substituted)
½ Pint heavy cream
3 Tablespoons granulated sugar

Directions

Melt the sweet and bitter chocolate in 3 tablespoons of heavy cream. (Grandma would have used the back burner of the coal stove for this. You may use the top of a double boiler over boiling water.) Beat the butter and confectioners' sugar into the hot chocolate. Place half of this chocolate icing in a small bowl and save it to use later when assembling the cake. To the chocolate that remains in the pan, add ½ cup of granulated sugar, the egg yolks, and the milk. Mix well. Cook over boiling water until the pudding is quite thick. Strain the pudding and chill it for one hour. Stir in the vanilla.

TO ASSEMBLE

Assemble a 9-inch spring-form pan and line the bottom with ladyfingers. Sprinkle these with half of the sherry. Spread with half of the chilled pudding. Crumble 9 macaroons evenly over the pudding. Dribble half of the reserved bitter and sweet chocolate icing over the macaroons. Arrange ladyfingers neatly over this and sprinkle with the remaining sherry. Continue as above with layers of pudding and macaroon crumbs. Whip the heavy cream with 3 tablespoons of sugar and pipe it in peaks over the top of the dessert. Dribble the remaining chocolate icing decoratively over the top of the cake. Chill for 3 hours.

macaroon
cake

(Serves 12 to 14)

This moist white cake has bits of macaroon in each layer but, more importantly, it has a soft, sweet filling of macaroons flavored with Crème de Cacao. The frosting is fluffy and marshmallowy, and it is sprinkled with grated chocolate. Yum.

CAKE
Ingredients

2 Cups cake flour, measured after
    sifting
3 Teaspoons baking powder
½ Teaspoon salt
½ Cup butter
1 Cup granulated sugar
2 Eggs
¾ Cup milk
1 Teaspoon vanilla extract
½ Cup dry macaroon crumbs

Directions

Sift together the sifted flour, the baking powder, and the salt. Cream the butter and sugar thoroughly. Beat in the eggs, one at a time, beating well after each addition. Stir in the dry ingredients, alternately with the milk, mixing enough to blend the ingredients thoroughly, but do not beat the batter. Add the vanilla extract. Mix gently. Grease and flour two 8-inch cake pans. Sprinkle half of the macaroon crumbs evenly into each pan. Spoon half of the batter into the center of each pan. Carefully spread the batter to the edge of the pan, so as not to disturb the macaroon crumbs. Bake for 25 to 30 minutes in an oven preheated to 375 degrees F. Cool.

MACAROON FILLING
Ingredients

2 Cups macaroon crumbs
⅓ Cup crème de cacao
⅓ Cup granulated sugar
⅔ Cup water

Directions

Place all ingredients in a saucepan and boil, stirring constantly until the excess liquid has boiled away and the filling is quite stiff. Cool.

MARSHMALLOW FROSTING (Frost the cake not more than one hour before serving, since this icing may wilt if it stands too long.)
Ingredients

¾ Cup granulated sugar
⅛ Teaspoon cream of tartar
1 Egg white
⅓ Cup boiling water
1 Teaspoon crème de cacao

Directions

Fill a small mixing bowl with hot water and let it stand while you assemble and measure the above ingredients. Empty the bowl of water quickly; dry it; and add the sugar, the cream of tartar, and the egg white. Beat for a few seconds and then add the boiling water. Continue to beat until the frosting stands in stiff peaks when you raise the beater blades. Beat in the crème de cacao.

TO ASSEMBLE THE CAKE

Slice a thin slice from the cooled layers, if it is necessary to level them. Spread the bottom layer with Macaroon Filling, top with the second layer, and frost with Marshmallow Frosting. Sprinkle with grated sweet or semi-sweet chocolate. Refrigerate until serving time.

chocolate-pecan
upside-down
cake

(Serves 12 to 16)

Are you searching for a dessert that is sure to delight children as well as adults? Search no more, for this cake has chocolate to please the toddlers and a caramel-pecan top to please the grownups.

PECAN TOPPING

Ingredients

⅓ Cup butter
⅓ Cup dark brown sugar
1 Cup pecan halves
¾ Cup corn syrup

Directions

Cream the butter and the brown sugar. Stir in the nuts and the corn syrup. Grease a 9- by 12-inch cake pan. Spread the pecan mixture evenly over the bottom of the pan.

CAKE
Ingredients

6 Tablespoons butter
1¼ Cups granulated sugar
2 Eggs
4 Ounces bitter chocolate
1 Teaspoon vanilla
2 Cups all-purpose flour
2 Teaspoons baking powder
1½ Cups milk

Directions

Cream the butter. Add the sugar very gradually, mixing well after each addition. Separate the egg yolks from the whites. Reserve the whites. Beat the yolks into the butter-sugar mixture. Place the chocolate in the top of a double boiler. Melt over boiling water. Cool the chocolate to room temperature and add it, with the vanilla, to the cake mixture. Sift the flour with the baking powder, and add the dry ingredients to the chocolate mixture, alternately with the milk, beginning and ending with the dry ingredients. Beat the egg whites until they hold a point and fold them into the batter. Spread the batter carefully and evenly over the pecans and bake for 50 minutes in an oven preheated to 350 degrees F., or until the cake springs back when the center is pressed gently with the finger. Immediately invert the cake on a serving platter and remove the pan. Cool to room temperature. *Do not chill.* Serve with daubs of vanilla ice cream topped with sweet chocolate sauce.

SWEET CHOCOLATE SAUCE
Ingredients

4 Ounces sweet chocolate
2 Tablespoons butter
½ Cup granulated sugar

¾ Cup light cream
1 Teaspoon vanilla

Directions

Place chocolate squares and butter in a small heavy skillet. Melt over a low flame. Combine sugar and cream in a mixing bowl. Add to the melted chocolate. Stir over a medium-low flame until the sauce reaches the boiling point. Reduce the heat. Cook over a low flame until the sauce thickens somewhat. Stir in the vanilla. Serve hot.

mocha
ladyfinger
cake

(Serves 12 to 16)

Everyone knows that coffee and cream are a marvelous combination. Here's a recipe that features these flavor favorites in company with ladyfingers and crème de cacao.

Ingredients

2 Envelopes unflavored gelatin
½ Cup extra-strength cold coffee
1 Cup confectioners' sugar
1 Cup milk
2 Tablespoons crème de cacao
2 Egg whites
2½ Cups heavy cream
50 Ladyfingers
½ Cup crème de cacao
2 Tablespoons heavy cream
5 Tablespoons granulated sugar
½ Teaspoon vanilla extract
¼ Cup chocolate sprinkles

Directions

Soften the gelatin in the cold coffee. Combine the sugar and milk in the top of a double boiler and cook over boiling water until it is hot. Add the gelatin and stir until it is dissolved. Cool to room temperature. Add the 2 tablespoons of crème de cacao and beat the mixture until it is light. Beat the egg whites until they stand in stiff peaks and fold them into the coffee mixture along with 1½ cups of whipped heavy cream.

Mix ½ cup of crème de cacao, 2 tablespoons of heavy cream, and 2 tablespoons of granulated sugar until the sugar is dissolved.

TO ASSEMBLE THE CAKE

Line the bottom of a spring-form pan with wax paper. Cover the paper with half of the ladyfingers. Sprinkle the ladyfingers liberally with the crème de cacao mixture. Pour half of the coffee mixture onto these. Chill for 2 hours. Arrange the remaining ladyfingers on the coffee mixture, sprinkle liberally with the crème de cacao mixture, top with the remaining coffee mixture, and chill for 2 hours. Remove the sides of the pan.

Whip the remaining cup of heavy cream with 3 tablespoons of granulated sugar until it is fairly stiff. Stir in the vanilla extract. Sprinkle the top of the cake with chocolate sprinkles. Ice the sides of the cake with flavored whipped cream. Use a pastry tube to pipe a row of whipped cream rosettes around the rim of the cake. Chill until serving time.

fudge cake

Super dark and rich is this double-frosted Fudge Cake.

CAKE

Ingredients

2½ Cups granulated sugar
4½ Squares unsweetened chocolate
1½ Cups milk
¼ Cup butter
½ Cup vegetable shortening
2 Teaspoons vanilla extract
½ Teaspoon red food coloring
5 Eggs
1½ Teaspoons soda
½ Teaspoon salt
3 Cups all-purpose flour
¼ Cup Cherry Marnier

Directions

Place the chocolate, 1 cup of sugar, and ¾ cup of milk in a saucepan. Cook, stirring constantly until the chocolate is melted. Cool to room temperature. Mix the butter and the shortening. Add the remaining sugar, and cream the mixture until it is light and puffy. Add the vanilla extract and the food coloring. Add the eggs, one at a time, beating well after each addition. Sift the soda, salt, and flour together. Add the dry ingredients to the butter and egg mixture alternately with the remaining milk and the Cherry Marnier. Beat well after each addition. Stir in the chocolate mixture until no dark-brown streaks may be seen. Pour the batter into three greased 9-inch layer cake pans. Bake at 350 degrees F. until the cake bounces back when pressed lightly with the finger. Cool.

CHOCOLATE FROSTING
Ingredients

6 Ounces sweet chocolate
¼ Cup water
1 Tablespoon granulated sugar
4 Egg yolks
½ Cup butter
½ Teaspoon vanilla extract

Directions

Place the chocolate, the water, and the sugar in the top of a double boiler. Stir until the chocolate has melted and the mixture is smooth. Beat in the egg yolks one at a time. Cook over boiling water for 3 minutes, stirring constantly. Cool to lukewarm, and stir in the vanilla extract.

PENUCHE ICING
Ingredients

1 Cup butter
2¼ Cups light brown sugar, tightly packed
½ Cup milk
3 Cups confectioners' sugar
¾ Cup toasted slivered almonds
4 Candied cherries

Directions

Melt the butter. Add the brown sugar. Boil the mixture for 2 minutes over low heat, stir in the milk and continue to boil, stirring constantly. Cool to lukewarm. Sift the confectioners' sugar, and add it gradually to the sugar-butter mixture. If the icing seems thin, place pan in ice water and stir until the icing is thick enough to spread.

TO ASSEMBLE THE CAKE

Place one cake layer on a cake plate, ice with the Penuche Icing, and sprinkle with the toasted almonds. Continue in this manner until the entire cake is assembled. Ice the sides of the cake with chocolate frosting, reserving a bit to decorate the top of the cake. Press toasted almonds on the side of the cake. Decorate the center of the top of the cake with loops of chocolate frosting pressed through a fluted pastry tube. Place half a candied cherry in each loop.

tangerine cake*

(Serves 12 to 16)

Serve this delicate cake at a formal dinner party or as an elegant aftermath to a birthday or anniversary party. It is a dessert that is sure to be remembered.

FONDANT ICING
Ingredients

2 Cups granulated sugar
¼ Teaspoon cream of tartar

1 Cup boiling water
2 Tablespoons Grand Marnier

Directions

(If you don't own a candy thermometer, now is a good time to buy one. It makes cooking icings and candies ridiculously easy by removing the element of doubt.) Mix the sugar and the cream of tartar until the cream of tartar is no longer visible. Add the boiling water and stir until the sugar dissolves. Boil this syrup without stirring, until it spins a thread, or until the candy thermometer registers 234 degrees F. Wipe the inside of the pan to remove the hardened sugar. Pour the fondant into an enamel cake pan (or onto a marble or enamel surface) and quickly work it with a spatula until it is frosty white and smooth. Knead it for a moment and then store it for 2 days in an airtight container in the refrigerator.

When your cake is ready to be iced, place the fondant in the top of a double boiler and heat over 1 inch of simmering water for 2 minutes. Add the 2 tablespoons of Grand Marnier and stir well. Continue to thin with Grand Marnier until the icing is proper spreading consistency.

CAKE
Ingredients

⅓ Cup plus 2 tablespoons granulated sugar
9 Egg yolks
½ Cup ground hazelnuts

2 Small tangerines
1½ Cups all-purpose flour
8 Egg whites
3 Tablespoons granulated sugar

* Prepare the fondant icing 2 days in advance of serving.

162

Directions

Beat ⅓ cup plus 2 tablespoons of granulated sugar with the egg yolks until they are light lemon in color. Add the hazelnuts and the juice from the tangerines. Sift the flour and stir it in gradually. Beat the egg whites until they are stiff. Add 3 tablespoons of sugar and continue to beat for 1 minute. Fold the sweetened egg whites into the batter. Divide between three buttered cake pans, set the baking pans on a baking sheet or a double thickness of aluminum foil, and bake in an oven preheated to 375 degrees F. for about 45 minutes, or until they test done. Cool.

TO ASSEMBLE THE CAKE

Ingredients

1 Cup heavy cream
4 Tablespoons granulated sugar
1 Tablespoon Grand Marnier
30 Tangerine sections
½ Cup granulated sugar
3 Tablespoons water

Directions

Whip the cream until it holds a soft peak. Sprinkle in 4 tablespoons of sugar, a little at a time, and continue beating until the cream is fairly stiff. Stir in the Grand Marnier. Chill.

Use a sharp, large knife to trim the layers evenly and reserve the best one for the top. Spread the first and second layers with the flavored whipped cream and top with the third layer, reserving ¼ cup of the whipped cream for decoration. Thin the fondant icing as directed. Ice the cake by pouring the icing onto the top layer, smoothing it with a large spatula or knife, and spreading it as it runs down the sides. Keep working the icing until the cake is wrapped in a smooth coating of thin, white fondant. Pull the white threads from the tangerine sections and gently squeeze out the seeds with the thumb and forefinger. Be careful not to damage the sections of fruit. Bring ½ cup of sugar and 3 tablespoons of water to a boil. Boil for 2 minutes, remove from the flame, and carefully stir in the tangerine sections. Drain the fruit and cool to room temperature. Arrange the tangerine sections in a circle about an inch from the edge of the cake, overlapping them slightly. Use a pastry tube to pipe tiny rosettes of whipped cream around the inside of the circle of fruit and around the bottom of the cake. Chill until ready to serve.

raspberry cake with chocolate filling

(Serves 12 to 16)

This is a very special cake that is time consuming but not tricky to prepare. My suggestion is this: Prepare it the day before your next dinner party, refrigerate it until time to serve, and then accept compliments with great modesty.

CAKE
Ingredients

5 Egg yolks
½ Cup granulated sugar
¼ Cup ground almonds
¼ Cup all-purpose flour
3 Egg whites
½ Lemon
3 Drops almond extract
3 Drops red food coloring

Directions

Cream the eggs and the sugar until they are light and fluffy. Stir in the ground almonds and the flour. Beat the egg whites until they hold a stiff peak. Fold the beaten egg whites into the egg-nut mixture. Squeeze and strain the juice of ½ lemon. Add the lemon juice, the almond extract, and the food coloring to the batter. Mix gently, but well. Bake in a buttered 9-inch cake pan in an oven preheated to 350 degrees F. for 25 to 30 minutes or until the center of the cake springs back when lightly pressed with the finger. Cool.

ALMOND SHORT PASTE
Ingredients

1⅓ Cups all-purpose flour
¼ Cup plus 2 tablespoons granulated sugar
¼ Cup ground blanched almonds
½ Cup butter
2 Small eggs
¼ Teaspoon vanilla extract

Directions

Sift the flour and the sugar together onto a pastry board. Sprinkle the ground almonds over the mound of flour, and make a well in the center about 4 inches in diameter. Put into the depression the butter (cut into flakes) and the eggs and the vanilla. Use your fingers to blend the butter and eggs to a liquid state. Gradually gather in the flour around the edges of the well and mix quickly with the fingers to form a smooth dough. Chill the dough and then roll it into a circle 9 inches in diameter and ⅓ inch thick. Press this into the bottom of a 9-inch assembled spring-form pan. Bake at 350 degrees F. for 25 to 30 minutes or until it is lightly browned.

Cool in the pan ½ hour and gently loosen around the edge with a knife but do not remove the sides of the pan.

CHOCOLATE FILLING
Ingredients

4 Ounces German sweet chocolate
1 Cup milk
½ Cup sugar
1 Tablespoon unflavored gelatin

¼ Cup water
3 Egg yolks
½ Teaspoon vanilla extract
1 Cup heavy cream

Directions

Place the chocolate, the milk, and the sugar in a saucepan and mix over medium heat until the chocolate is melted. Sprinkle the gelatin over the cool water, allow it to soften for a few moments, and then add it to the hot chocolate mixture. Stir until the gelatin is dissolved. Add the egg yolks and the vanilla and beat until smooth. Cool to room temperature. Meanwhile, whip the heavy cream until it stands in a fairly stiff peak. Fold the whipped cream into the cooled chocolate mixture.

TO ASSEMBLE THE CAKE
Ingredients

2 Cups raspberry jelly or jam
½ Cup chocolate sprinkles

1 Cup heavy cream
17 Fresh raspberries (if in season)

Directions

Strain the raspberry jelly to remove the seeds. Spread the cooled Almond Short Paste with ⅓ cup of the jelly. Split the layer of cake to form two thin layers. Place one layer on the jelly-covered Almond Short Paste. Adjust the rim of the spring-form pan and spread the Chocolate Filling over the thin layer of cake. Chill for at least an hour. Remove the rim of the pan. Add the second cake layer. Spread the top and the sides of the assembled cake with the remaining raspberry jelly. Chill overnight. About an hour before the cake is to be served, press the chocolate sprinkles evenly over the top and the sides of the cake. Refrigerate. Whip the heavy cream until it is quite stiff. Remove the cake from the refrigerator and use a pastry tube to pipe peaks of whipped cream around the top and base of the cake. If fresh raspberries are in season, place them in a small rosette of whipped cream in the center of the cake and at regular intervals around the rim of the cake. Chill until time to serve.

pineapple ambrosia cake

(Serves 12 to 14)

"Luscious" is the word to describe this frothy Pineapple Ambrosia Cake. A subtle combination of fresh pineapple and orange slices forms the filling for this moist, white cake. The frosting is flavored with orange and sprinkled with shredded coconut to complete a cake that is sure to be enjoyed by adults and children alike.

CAKE

Ingredients

2 Cups cake flour, measured
after sifting
3 Teaspoons baking powder
½ Teaspoon salt
½ Cup butter
1 Cup granulated sugar
2 Eggs
¾ Cup milk
½ Cup dry macaroon crumbs
1 Teaspoon vanilla extract

Directions

Sift together the sifted flour, the baking powder, and the salt. Cream the butter until it is light and fluffy, and add the sugar a bit at a time. Cream the butter and sugar thoroughly. Beat in the eggs, one at a time, beating well after each addition. Stir in the flour mixture alternately with the milk, mixing enough to blend the ingredients thoroughly, but do not beat the batter. Stir in the vanilla extract. Grease and flour two 8-inch cake pans. Sprinkle half the macaroon crumbs evenly into each pan. Spoon half the batter into the center of each pan. Carefully spread the batter to the edge of the pan so as not to disturb the macaroon crumbs. Bake for 25 to 30 minutes in an oven preheated to 375 degrees F. Cool.

PINEAPPLE FILLING
Ingredients

1 Cup fresh pineapple, peeled,
  cored, and chopped
¼ Cup canned or fresh pineapple
  juice
1 Cup granulated sugar
1 Envelope unflavored gelatin
¼ Cup water

Directions

Peel, core, and chop the pineapple. Cook the pineapple, the pineapple juice, and the sugar over low heat for 10 minutes. Soften the gelatin by sprinkling it over the water, and stir it into the hot pineapple mixture. Cool to room temperature.

CREAM FILLING
Ingredients

1 Cup milk
2 Tablespoons all-purpose flour
2 Egg yolks
2 Tablespoons granulated sugar
1 Teaspoon vanilla extract

Directions

Mix the milk, the flour, the egg yolks, and the sugar in the top of a double boiler. Cook over boiling water, stirring constantly, until the cream is thick. Do not overcook or the cream will curdle. Cool to room temperature. Stir in the vanilla extract and the pineapple mixture, and chill.

MARSHMALLOW FROSTING (Frost the cake an hour before serving. This icing may wilt if it stands too long.)

Ingredients

¾ Cup granulated sugar
⅛ Teaspoon cream of tartar
1 Egg white
⅓ Cup boiling water
1 Teaspoon orange extract
4 Drops yellow food coloring
½ Teaspoon almond extract

Directions

Fill a small mixing bowl with hot water and let it stand while you assemble and measure the above ingredients. Empty the bowl and quickly add the sugar, the cream of tartar, and the egg white. Beat for a few seconds and then add the boiling water. Stir in the orange extract and the food coloring. Continue to beat until the frosting stands in stiff peaks when you raise the beater blades. Beat in the almond extract.

TO ASSEMBLE THE CAKE (No more than one hour before serving time.)

Ingredients

30 Peeled wedges of orange
Grated coconut

Directions

Slice a thin slice from the top of one layer to level it. Spread this layer with the chilled Pineapple-Cream Filling. Arrange 15 peeled orange wedges on the filling, and top with the second layer. Frost the cake with the Marshmallow Frosting, arrange the remaining orange slices attractively around the top of the cake, and sprinkle the sides with the grated coconut. Chill until serving time.

blackberry
jam
cake

(Serves 12 to 16)

A crumbly blackberry jam cake similar to the one grandma used to bake just might provide the perfect dessert for that special family gathering, or perhaps for a ladies' club luncheon.

CAKE

Ingredients

½ Cup butter
1 Cup dark brown sugar
4 Eggs
2 Cups all-purpose flour
1 Teaspoon baking soda
¾ Teaspoon cinnamon
¾ Teaspoon nutmeg
½ Teaspoon ground cloves
½ Teaspoon allspice
3 Tablespoons milk
½ Teaspoon lemon juice
1 Cup seedless blackberry jam
1¼ Cups chopped dates

Directions

Cream the butter and the brown sugar until the mixture is light and fluffy. Separate the eggs. Beat the egg yolks and add them to the butter-sugar mixture. Stir well. Sift the flour. Add to it the baking soda and the spices, and sift once more. Mix the milk and lemon juice in a cup and place it in the oven for a few seconds until the milk curdles. Mix the sour milk and the blackberry jam. Stir the dry ingredients into the creamed mixture, alternately with the jam mixture. Mix thoroughly. Dust the chopped dates with a little flour and add them to the batter. Beat the egg whites until they are stiff, and fold them in.

Pour the batter into two oiled 8-inch cake pans and bake in an oven preheated to 375 degrees F. for 30 minutes, or until the layers begin to pull away from the sides of the pans. Cool on a wire rack.

ICING

Ingredients

¼ Cup butter
1 Box (3½ cups) confectioners' sugar
⅛ Teaspoon salt
4 Tablespoons heavy cream
1 Teaspoon almond extract
2 Tablespoons seedless raspberry jam
4 Drops red food coloring

Directions

Cut the butter into thin slices and allow it to come to room temperature. Mix the sugar and salt. Cream the butter and one cup of the sugar until it is smooth. Add the remaining sugar alternately with the cream. Stir in the almond extract. Reserve ¼ cup of this white icing for decoration. Stir the raspberry jam and the food coloring into the icing remaining in the bowl. Ice the cake with this pale pink icing and use a pastry tube to pipe an edge of the reserved white icing around the rim of the cake.

coconut chocolate cake

(Serves 12 to 16)

Just the dessert to turn a meat-and-potatoes meal into a gourmet repast. Begin with a cake-y chocolate layer, heap on a frothy coconut-flavored cream, top with grated coconut, and chill. Then, serve with pride.

CAKE
Ingredients

2 Squares (2 ounces) semi-sweet
    chocolate
¾ Cup granulated sugar
5 Egg yolks
⅓ Cup ground Brazil nuts
¼ Cup all-purpose flour
3 Egg whites
1 Teaspoon vanilla extract
1 Teaspoon lemon juice

Directions

Place chocolate in the top of a double boiler and melt over boiling water. Stir in ¼ cup of sugar and cook, stirring constantly, for 3 minutes. Cool to room temperature. Cream the egg yolks with ½ cup of sugar. Stir in the ground nuts and the flour. Add the cooled chocolate and stir until no dark-brown streaks of chocolate can be seen. Beat the egg whites until they stand in stiff peaks. Fold the beaten egg whites into the chocolate mixture. Add the vanilla and the lemon juice and continue to fold until no egg white can be seen. Spread the batter in a buttered 9-inch spring-form pan. Bake at 350 degrees F. for 35 minutes. Cool the cake in the pan.

COCONUT CREAM
Ingredients

2 Eight-ounce cans sweetened shredded coconut
2 Cups milk
⅓ Cup granulated sugar
¼ Cup water
2 Tablespoons unflavored gelatin
3 Egg yolks
½ Teaspoon almond extract
1 Cup heavy cream

Directions

Bring the milk to a boil and remove from the flame. Stir in the shredded coconut and the sugar while the milk is still hot. Allow the coconut to steep in the hot milk for 10 minutes. Reheat and strain the milk, pressing the coconut to remove as much flavor as possible. Soften the gelatin in the water for a few minutes and dissolve it in the hot coconut milk. Cool to room temperature. Beat the egg yolks lightly and add them, with the almond extract, to the cooled coconut milk. Chill until the mixture thickens slightly, by stirring frequently. Whip the heavy cream until it is fairly stiff. Fold it into the chilled coconut mixture. (Make sure the rim of the spring-form pan is firmly in place.) Spread the coconut cream over the cake and chill for 2 hours.

TO ASSEMBLE THE CAKE
Ingredients

1 Cup heavy cream
3 Tablespoons grated sweet chocolate
½ Cup shredded coconut
8 Candied cherries

Directions

Carefully remove the rim of the spring-form pan. Whip the cream until it is quite stiff. Use a pastry tube to pipe ridges of whipped cream around the sides and the top of the cake. Sprinkle the entire top of the cake and the whipped cream ridges with finely grated chocolate. Place a circle of shredded coconut approximately two inches from the outer rim of the top of the cake. Cut the cherries in half and place them round side up at regular intervals between the outer edge of the cake and the circle of shredded coconut. Chill until time to serve.

swedish apple-spice cake

(Serves 12 to 16)

Apples and spice and everything nice go into this whipped-cream-topped cake.

APPLE FILLING

Ingredients

10 Medium-small tart apples
1 Cup granulated sugar
1 Cup water
¼ Cup Grand Marnier
¼ Cup sherry
½ Teaspoon freshly grated cinnamon
¼ Teaspoon freshly grated nutmeg
1 Tablespoon lemon juice
2 Tablespoons maple syrup

Directions

Peel, core, and cut the apples into quarters. Place the sugar, the water, the Grand Marnier, the sherry, the cinnamon, and the nutmeg in a saucepan. Cook 5 to 6 minutes. Turn the apples into this syrup and poach them until they are tender. Use a slotted spoon to place the apples in a dish. Add the lemon juice and maple syrup to the juices remaining in the saucepan. Cook this mixture over low heat until it is fairly thick. Replace the apples in the saucepan. Stir.

CAKE

Ingredients

¾ Cup butter	1 Teaspoon freshly grated nutmeg
1⅓ Cups granulated sugar	1 Teaspoon freshly grated cinnamon
2 Egg yolks	½ Teaspoon baking soda
⅞ Cup milk	½ Teaspoon ground cloves
1½ Teaspoons lemon juice	½ Teaspoon salt
2 Cups all-purpose flour	2 Egg whites
1 Teaspoon baking powder	

Directions

Cream the butter. Gradually add the sugar and beat until the mixture is light and fluffy. Beat the egg yolks and stir into the creamed butter and sugar. Add the lemon juice to the milk and allow it to stand for a few minutes in a warm place. Sift flour twice with the baking powder, the nutmeg, the cinnamon, the baking soda, the cloves, and the salt. Add the dry ingredients alternately with the soured milk, beating the batter until it is smooth after each addition. Beat the egg whites stiff but not dry, and fold them gently but thoroughly into the batter. Turn the batter into a lightly greased and floured 11-inch tube pan. Drop heaping tablespoonfuls of the apple mixture into the batter until the apples are all used up. Bake in a moderate oven (350 degrees F.) for 1 hour, or until a toothpick inserted into the cake (not the apple filling) comes out clean. Cool 15 minutes. Loosen cake around the sides and center tube with a sharp knife. Turn upside down on a cake plate.

TOPPING

Ingredients

1 Pint heavy cream
2 Tablespoons granulated sugar

Directions

Whip the cream and the sugar together. Heap whipped cream on top of the cake. Serve immediately.

VARIATION

This cake is also delicious topped with ice cream and sprinkled with nutmeg.

coffeecake with poppy seed filling

(Serves 12 to 16)

A coffeecake for a special occasion is this attractive ring filled with swirls of sweetened poppy seeds and raisins.

COFFEECAKE
Ingredients

2 Envelopes of yeast	⅔ Cup granulated sugar
¼ Cup water	1 Teaspoon salt
¾ Cup milk	4 Cups all-purpose flour measured after sifting
¼ Cup cream	2 Eggs
6 Tablespoons butter	1 Teaspoon cinnamon

Directions

Sprinkle the yeast over ¼ cup lukewarm water that has been placed in a fairly large, flat bowl. Scald the milk and the cream together and place in a large mixing bowl with 5 tablespoons of butter (retain the sixth tablespoon for later use), the sugar, and ½ teaspoon of salt. Cool to lukewarm and stir in 2 cups minus 2 tablespoons of sifted flour. This should produce a sticky batter, not a dough. When the yeast has softened completely, stir it alternately with the beaten eggs into the sticky batter. Beat thoroughly. Sift together the remaining flour and ½ teaspoon of salt. Stir enough of this flour into the batter to produce a soft dough. If the dough is still a little sticky, add flour until it can be handled without sticking to the fingers. Turn the dough onto a lightly floured board and knead by folding one edge of the dough inward and pressing down firmly with the knuckles. Turn the dough and repeat the process. Continue to knead until the dough is smooth and has a satin sheen. (This should take about 15 minutes of *vigorous* kneading.) Place the dough in a buttered bowl, cover with a clean tea towel, and let the dough rise for 2 hours in a place that is warm and free from drafts. Meanwhile, prepare the Poppy Seed Filling.

POPPY SEED FILLING

Ingredients

½ Cup poppy seeds
½ Cup raisins
6 Tablespoons granulated sugar

¼ Cup milk
1 Tablespoon lemon juice

Directions

Whirl the poppy seeds in a blender for a few minutes, stopping the machine several times and stirring to bring the uncracked seeds to the top. Plump the raisins by covering them with boiling water for 5 minutes. Drain the raisins, chop them coarsely, and place them in a saucepan with the poppy seed powder, the sugar, and the milk. Simmer over *low* heat for 5 minutes, stirring constantly. Add the lemon juice and cook the mixture for 1 minute more, or until it is very thick. Cool to room temperature.

TO ASSEMBLE THE COFFEECAKE

When the dough is light and has doubled in bulk, roll it into a rectangle ½ inch thick. Melt the remaining tablespoon of butter and brush the dough with it. Sprinkle with cinnamon and sugar and spread with the cooled poppy seed filling. Roll like a jelly roll and bend the rolled dough around into a ring. Pinch the ends of the roll together with thumb and forefinger. Place the ring on a buttered baking sheet and cut it from the top to within ½ inch of the bottom in slices at 1-inch intervals around the cake. Bend each slice slightly to the side. The result will be an attractive ring with "pinwheels" of dough bent to reveal swirls of poppy seed filling. Cover with a tea towel and once again let the ring rise in a warm, draft-free place, until it is double in bulk. Bake for 25 to 35 minutes in an oven preheated to 350 degrees F. While the coffeecake is still warm, ice it with the following:

CONFECTIONERS' SUGAR ICING

Ingredients

1 Cup confectioners' sugar
¼ Cup water

1 Egg white

Directions

Mix the sugar and the water until smooth. Beat the egg white until it is frothy, and add the sugar mixture. Beat at high speed for several minutes. Ice the top of the coffeecake, allowing the icing to drip over the edges and run down the sides of the cake. Serve with sweet butter.

norwegian nut torte

(Serves 12 to 16)

This nut torte is quite uncommon, and it is uncommonly delicious. The crunchy walnut layers are saturated with a light, honey syrup, and then chilled and spread with a rum-flavored cream cheese topping. I recommend it highly.

NUT TORTE
Ingredients

2 Cups chopped walnuts
2 Cups crushed zwieback crumbs
2 Teaspoons baking powder
1¼ Teaspoons cinnamon
¼ Teaspoon powdered anise
¼ Teaspoon salt
2 Teaspoons vanilla extract
7 Eggs
1 Cup granulated sugar

Directions

Mix thoroughly the chopped nuts, the zwieback crumbs, the baking powder, the cinnamon, the anise, the salt, and the vanilla extract. Separate the eggs and beat the yolks into the nut mixture. Beat the egg whites until they are foamy, and continue beating while you sprinkle in the sugar. Beat until stiff, then fold the meringue into the batter. Grease three round 9-inch cake pans, divide the batter among them, and bake for 30 minutes in an oven preheated to 325 degrees F. Carefully loosen the layers and remove them from the pan while they are still warm, but not hot. Cool on separate plates.

HONEY SYRUP
Ingredients

3 Cups water
1 Cup honey
1 Cup sugar

Directions

Boil the syrup over a medium flame for 30 minutes. Cool to room temperature.

CHEESE TOPPING
Ingredients

16 Ounces cream cheese
4 Egg yolks
¾ Cup granulated sugar
3 Tablespoons rum

Directions

Cream the cream cheese thoroughly in the small bowl of an electric mixer. Beat the egg yolks in another bowl. Add the sugar and the rum, and continue beating for 1 minute. Pour the egg yolk mixture into the cream cheese, in a thin steady stream, beating constantly. Beat until smooth.

TO ASSEMBLE THE TORTE
Ingredients

16 Walnut halves

Directions

Pour one-third of the Honey Syrup over each layer and allow them to soak in the refrigerator for 4 hours. Slip one honey-soaked layer onto a cake plate and cover with the Cheese Topping, allowing some topping to drip over the edges. Continue the process until all of the layers and the Cheese Topping are used up. Decorate the top of the torte with 16 walnut halves. Chill for several hours or overnight. Serve cold.

striped chocolate pudding pie

(Serves 12 to 16)

Here's an attractive dessert you really should try if you are at all addicted to chocolate. It's more than a pudding, it's more than a pie, and it utilizes a delicate chocolate cream to combine the best features of each.

CRUST

Ingredients

2½ Cups all-purpose flour
1¼ Teaspoons salt
15 Tablespoons shortening
10 to 12 Tablespoons ice water

Directions

Sift the flour and the salt into a mixing bowl. Cut in the shortening with a pastry blender or two knives, until the particles are the size of small peas. Sprinkle in 8 tablespoons of ice water while tossing with a fork. If the dough is not moist enough to form a ball, sprinkle in another tablespoon of ice water. Toss again. If necessary, add another tablespoon of water. Do not add too much water or the dough will become sticky. Chill for 20 minutes. Roll out the pastry on a floured surface to a circle 9¼ inches by not quite ¼ inch thick and fit it into the bottom of an assembled 9-inch spring-form pan. Prick with a fork and bake for 15 minutes in an oven preheated to 450 degrees F. Cool in the pan.

FILLING
Ingredients

1¼ Cups granulated sugar
3¾ Tablespoons cornstarch
10 Egg yolks
5 Cups milk
2½ Tablespoons unflavored gelatin

½ Cup water
2 Squares unsweetened chocolate
2 Squares semi-sweet chocolate
2 Teaspoons vanilla extract
½ Cup hazelnuts

Directions

Mix the sugar and the cornstarch. Add the egg yolks and mix thoroughly. Scald the milk and stir it into the egg yolk mixture. Pour this into the top of a double boiler and cook over boiling water, stirring constantly until the custard is thick enough to coat a spoon. Do not overcook or the custard will curdle. Sprinkle the gelatin over the water and 1 teaspoon vanilla, and stir. Reserve 1½ cups of this vanilla custard.

Place the chocolate in the top of a double boiler. Melt over boiling water. Cool the chocolate and stir in 1 teaspoon of the vanilla extract. Stir the larger portion of the custard into the melted chocolate. Mix thoroughly. Pour half of this chocolate custard into the cooled pie crust. Chill until firm. Keep the remaining chocolate custard at room temperature until needed. Meanwhile, finely crush or chop the hazelnuts and add all but 2 tablespoons of these to the reserved vanilla custard.

When the first layer of the chocolate filling is firm, cover with the vanilla custard-hazelnut mixture. Chill until firm.

Top this with the remaining chocolate custard. Once again, chill until firm. Remove the rim of the pan. Refrigerate.

TOPPING
Ingredients

1 Cup heavy cream
2 Tablespoons granulated sugar

3 Drops vanilla extract
2 Tablespoons chopped hazelnuts

Directions

Whip the cream until it holds a soft peak. Add the sugar and the vanilla and continue beating until the cream holds a fairly stiff peak. Place the whipped cream in a pastry bag. Use a fluted nozzle to pipe a thick edge of cream around the outside edge of the pie. Sprinkle the whipped cream with the chopped hazelnuts. Serve very cold.

cantaloupe pie

Fresh cantaloupe, orange cream, and apricot jam—what a marvelous combination of flavors.

KUCHEN CRUST
Ingredients

1 Cup all-purpose flour
2½ Tablespoons granulated sugar
⅛ Teaspoon salt
½ Cup butter
1 Egg yolk

Directions

Sift the dry ingredients together. Cut in the butter with a pastry cutter or two knives to produce a mealy mixture. Lightly beat the egg yolk in a cup and use a fork to stir it into the flour-butter mixture. With the back of a spoon, press the dough evenly into the bottom of a spring-form pan. Set the pan on the middle rack and bake at 350 degrees F. for 30 minutes. Remove from the oven and set on a wire rack. Cool in the pan.

ORANGE CREAM
Ingredients

¼ Cup granulated sugar
2½ Teaspoons potato starch
2 Egg yolks
¼ Cup apricot jam or preserves
1¼ Cups milk
1 Cup orange juice
⅓ Cup cold water
2 Envelopes unflavored gelatin
1 Cup heavy cream

Directions

Mix the sugar, the potato starch, and the egg yolks in a saucepan. Stir in the apricot jam. Add the milk and the orange juice, a little at a time. Cook over low heat, stirring constantly, until the mixture thickens. Soften the gelatin in the cold water, add this to the hot orange mixture, and stir until the gelatin is dissolved. Chill but do not allow to set completely. Whip the cream until it is stiff and fold it into the chilled, unset orange cream. Spread this mixture over the cooled Kuchen Crust and chill until the cream is set.

CANTALOUPE TOPPING

Ingredients

⅔ Cup apricot nectar
⅔ Cup apricot jam
2 Medium-sized cantaloupes
1 Tablespoon unflavored gelatin
3 Tablespoons cold water
6 or 7 Green candied cherries

Directions

Bring the apricot nectar and the apricot jam to a boil. Soften the gelatin in the cold water and stir it into the hot apricot syrup. Mix until the gelatin has completely dissolved.

Divide the first cantaloupe into halves the short way (as you would halve an orange). Remove seeds, peel, and then quarter each half. Now cut the fruit into slices, each approximately ¼ inch thick and two inches long.

Halve the second melon, discard the seeds and scoop out walnut-sized balls. Cut each ball in half.

Stir all of the cut cantaloupe, slices and small half-balls, into the apricot-gelatin mixture. Spoon the cantaloupe slices and syrup over the jellied orange cream, retaining the small half-balls in what is left of the apricot-gelatin mixture. Arrange the melon slices attractively. Now place the half melon balls, flat side down, on top of the pie around the outer edge so as to form a decorative border.

Cut the candied cherries into quarters and place one quarter around the edge of the pie where each of the half-melon balls meet.

watermelon
fruit
basket

(Serves 12 to 16)

Cut a watermelon into a fruit basket, garnish it with bunches of grapes and fill it with mixed fruits. You'll have a summertime treat that looks good enough to eat.

Ingredients

1 Small- to medium-sized watermelon
2 Cantaloupes
1 Honeydew melon
4 Bunches green grapes
2 Bunches purple grapes
6 Ripe peaches
2 Pounds Bing cherries
2 Cups blueberries
1 Cup granulated sugar

¾ Cup sherry
6 Maraschino cherries
20 Fresh mint leaves

Directions

Use a large sharp knife to cut two U-shaped sections from the top of the watermelon, leaving a 4-inch strip intact across the middle to form the handle of the "watermelon basket." With the point of the knife facing downward, cut around the edge of the melon, again leaving the center of the "handle" intact. Use a melon-ball cutter to cut all of the watermelon (from the cut inward) into melon balls. Scoop out any remaining pink melon bits from the bottom of the melon. Cut the pink melon remaining under the "handle" of the basket, but do not cut the handle itself. This should leave you with a "watermelon basket." Notch the top edges of the basket but do not disturb the "handle."

Cut the cantaloupe and the honeydew into balls. Peel the peaches, pit the cherries, and remove any stems from the blueberries and green grapes. Wash the fruit, being careful not to break up the bunches of purple grapes.

Place the watermelon, cantaloupe, and honeydew balls and peach slices in a bowl and sprinkle with the sugar and the sherry. Toss gently. Refrigerate all the fruit until an hour before serving time.

One hour prior to serving, place all of the fruit (except the 2 bunches of purple grapes) in the "watermelon basket." Gently toss the fruit. Use wooden hors d'oeuvre picks to fasten the 2 bunches of purple grapes to the "handle" of the "watermelon basket." Further decorate by placing wooden hors d'oeuvre picks through the maraschino cherries and 8 of the green grapes and pushing them in among the bunches of purple grapes. Tuck the peppermint leaves here and there among the bits of fruit in the "basket." Serve cold.

coconut
chocolate mousse

(Serves 12 to 16)

A chocolate mousse with a difference is this creamy but textured Coconut Chocolate Mousse. Prepare one day in advance of serving.

Ingredients

8 Egg yolks
1 Cup granulated sugar
15 Ounces semi-sweet chocolate
1¼ Teaspoons vanilla extract
1 Cup butter, softened
8 Egg whites
1 Cup chopped walnuts
1 Cup shredded dried coconut
1 Cup heavy cream

Directions

Beat the egg yolks and sugar at high speed until they are creamy and light lemon in color. Place the chocolate in the top of a double boiler. Melt over boiling water. Cool the melted chocolate to room temperature and add it, with the vanilla, to the egg-sugar mixture. Beat until smooth. Add the softened butter a bit at a time. Beat the egg whites until they hold a firm peak and fold them into the chocolate cream. Chop the walnuts and coconut into ¼-inch pieces. Fold 1 cup of the chopped coconut and walnuts into the chocolate mousse and pour into an oiled mold. Scatter the remaining cup of the chopped nut mixture over the mousse, pressing it down lightly. Chill overnight. An hour before serving, wrap the mold for a few seconds in towels moistened with hot water. Unmold onto a serving plate. Whip the cream until it begins to thicken.

Pipe whipped cream around the base, and in swirls over the top of the chilled mousse. Serve very cold.

syrian apricots*

(Serves 12 to 16)

This easy-to-prepare fruit dessert is unusually refreshing. The addition of rose water and whole blanched apricots adds an authentic near-Eastern flavor.

Ingredients

4 Eleven-ounce boxes fancy dried apricots
1½ Quarts canned apricot nectar
½ Cup granulated sugar
2½ Teaspoons rose water
2 Four-and-one-half-ounce cans whole blanched almonds

Directions

Wash the apricots, place them in a very large glass or plastic bowl. Mix apricot nectar, the sugar, and the rose water. Pour the liquid over the apricots and place in the refrigerator for 2 days. Stir occasionally. To serve, place the fruit and the liquid in a large glass dish and stir in the whole blanched almonds. Serve cold.

* Prepare the apricots 2 days in advance of serving.

strawberries
in
champagne

(Serves 12 to 16)

This is really a suggestion—not a recipe. Nothing complex here. Just fresh, ripe, beautiful strawberries served in a thin glass bowl, bubbling with champagne. Easy, but so cool and so special.

Ingredients

4 Quarts fresh, ripe strawberries
1 Bottle champagne (a vintage year, please)

Directions

Carefully remove the hulls from the strawberries. Place them in a large, thin glass bowl and cool them. Chill the champagne. Pour the champagne over the fruit at the table. Serve immediately in thin glass bowls.

index
to recipes